STUDIES

IN THE

SOCIAL ASPECTS

OF THE

DEPRESSION

Studies in the Social Aspects of the Depression

Advisory Editor: *ALEX BASKIN*

State University of New York at Stony Brook

RESEARCH MEMORANDUM ON SOCIAL ASPECTS OF RELIEF POLICIES IN THE DEPRESSION

By R. CLYDE WHITE

and
MARY K. WHITE

ARNO PRESS

A NEW YORK TIMES COMPANY

Reprint Edition 1972 by Arno Press Inc.

Reprinted from a copy in The Newark Public Library

LC# 70-162848
ISBN 0-405-00851-1

Studies in the Social Aspects of the Depression
ISBN for complete set: 0-405-00840-6
See last pages of this volume for titles.

Manufactured in the United States of America

Preface to the New Edition

WHEN NEWS OF THE STOCK MARKET CRASH traveled beyond the concrete canyons of lower Manhattan, few noninvestors dreamed that their lives would be disrupted and changed by the event. The news was as remote to most Americans as a volcanic eruption in Southern Europe or a tidal wave in the Far East. Few imagined that the waves set in motion in the last part of 1929 would reach into distant cities and towns and sweep them up in the turbulence and turmoil of unemployment, evictions, and foreclosures.

The nation was ill-prepared to relieve such widespread distress. Relief work was left to the philanthropic funds and foundations geared to assist the occasional victim of financial misfortune. These private efforts proved futile in the wake of the Wall Street disaster. Bread lines stretched far across city streets. The hungry rummaged through garbage cans in search of some edible morsels. Municipal assistance programs broke down as budgetary crisis followed budgetary crisis. It soon became clear that if men, women and children were to be saved from starvation, the federal government would have to intercede in their behalf.

R. Clyde White and Mary White have examined the problems associated with relief policies, traced the history of relief programs, described contemporary policies and practices, and inquired into the effectiveness of public and private agencies. They have raised a variety of questions regarding poverty and the pauperized and have suggested numerous research projects to deal with problems. Many of the issues which weighed heavily on the nation's mind during the years of the Depression are still with us. What is most anachronistic and troublesome is that even in times of affluence we have not learned to eradicate the persistent problem of poverty.

Alex Baskin
Stony Brook, New York, 1971

BULLETIN 38

1937

RESEARCH MEMORANDUM ON SOCIAL ASPECTS OF RELIEF POLICIES IN THE DEPRESSION

By R. CLYDE WHITE
Professor of Social Economics
School of Social Service Administration
University of Chicago &

MARY K. WHITE
Statistician
Chicago Council of Social Agencies

PREPARED UNDER THE DIRECTION OF THE
COMMITTEE ON STUDIES IN SOCIAL ASPECTS OF
THE DEPRESSION, WITH THE COOPERATION OF
THE COMMITTEE ON SOCIAL SECURITY

SOCIAL SCIENCE RESEARCH COUNCIL
230 PARK AVENUE   NEW YORK NY

The Social Science Research Council was organized in 1923 and formally incorporated in 1924, composed of representatives chosen from the seven constituent societies and from time to time from related disciplines such as law, geography, psychiatry, medicine, and others. It is the purpose of the Council to plan, foster, promote, and develop research in the social field.

CONSTITUENT ORGANIZATIONS

American Anthropological Association

American Economic Association

American Historical Association

American Political Science Association

American Psychological Association

American Sociological Society

American Statistical Association

FOREWORD

By the Committee on Studies in
Social Aspects of the Depression

THIS monograph on research pertaining to social aspects of relief policies in the depression is one of a series of thirteen sponsored by the Social Science Research Council to stimulate the study of depression effects on various social institutions.

The depression of the early 1930's was like the explosion of a bomb dropped in the midst of society. All major social institutions, such as government, family, church, and school, obviously were profoundly affected and the repercussions were so far-reaching that scarcely any type of human activity was untouched.

It would be valuable to have assembled the vast record of influence of this economic depression on society. Such a record would constitute an especially important preparation for meeting the shock of the next depression, if and when it comes. The facts about the impact of the depression on social life have been only partially recorded. Theories must be discussed and explored now, if much of the information to test them is not to be lost amid ephemeral sources.

The field is so broad that selection has been necessary. In keeping with its mandate from the Social Science Research Council, the Committee sponsored no studies of an exclusively economic or political nature. The subjects chosen for inclusion in the series were limited in number by available resources. The final selection was made from a much larger number of proposed subjects, on the basis of social importance and available personnel.

Although the monographs clearly reveal a uniformity of goal, they differ in the manner in which the various authors sought to attain that goal. This is a consequence of the Committee's belief that the promotion of research could best be served by not imposing rigid restrictions on the organization of materials by the contributors. It is felt that the encouraged freedom has resulted in the enrichment of the individual reports and of the series.

A common goal without rigidity in procedure was secured by requesting each author to examine critically the literature on the depression for the purpose of locating existing data and interpretations already reasonably well established, of discovering the more serious inadequacies in information, and of formulating research problems feasible for study. He was not expected to do this research himself. Nor was he expected to compile a full and systematically treated record of the depression as experienced in his field. Nevertheless, in indicating the new research which is needed, the writers found it necessary to report to some extent on what is known. These volumes actually contain much information on the social influences of the depression, in addition to their analyses of pressing research questions.

The undertaking was under the staff direction of Dr. Samuel A. Stouffer, who worked under the restrictions of a short time limit in order that prompt publication might be assured. He was assisted by Mr. Philip M. Hauser and Mr. A. J. Jaffe. The Committee wishes to express appreciation to the authors, who contributed their time and effort without remuneration, and to the many others who generously lent aid and materials.

The present monograph, by Dr. R. Clyde White and Mrs. Mary K. White, occupies a somewhat special place in the series. It was made possible through the cooperation of the Committee on Social Security of the Social Science Research Council, which provided funds and facilities enabling the senior author to do considerable traveling throughout the United States in order to gather impressions from relief officials and to explore sources of data which might be tapped in social research. To this Committee, to Dr. J. Frederic Dewhurst, its Director, and to Mr. Paul Webbink, Staff Member, special acknowledgment is due.

William F. Ogburn   Chairman
Shelby M. Harrison
Malcolm M. Willey

ACKNOWLEDGMENTS

THE writers are indebted to a great many people in many states for advice and for assistance in locating material for this study. Any effort to name all of them would be unsatisfactory. However, we should like to express appreciation of the financial assistance given by the Committee on Social Security of the Social Science Research Council and of the help of a few individuals who have given many hours of their time to discussing the problems of the study with us and to reading the manuscript. To Professor Samuel A. Stouffer of the University of Chicago, Dr. Howard B. Myers of the Works Progress Administration and Mr. Paul Webbink of the Committee on Social Security, we owe much for the privilege of frequent consultation and criticism of procedure. For reading the manuscript and offering many helpful suggestions we are grateful to: Professor Grace Abbott of the University of Chicago, Professor F. Stuart Chapin of the University of Minnesota, Miss Joanna C. Colcord of the Russell Sage Foundation, Dr. Neva Deardorff of the Welfare Council of New York City, Dr. Shelby M. Harrison of the Russell Sage Foundation, Mr. D. S. Howard of the Russell Sage Foundation, Dr. Ralph G. Hurlin of the Russell Sage Foundation and Professor Helen R. Wright of the University of Chicago.

Chicago, April, 1937   *The Authors*

CONTENTS

xi

Chapter I

The Basis of Plans for Research

RELIEF has been the biggest business in the country during the depression. It is the first time in our history that we have had a national relief policy and a national relief administration. European countries have been organizing and operating great systems of "social services" for more than a generation, but special circumstances in the United States have, up to 1929, reduced the need for comparable services and have prevented our seeing the problems which periodically arose in this country out of previous business depressions. The consequence of this lack of prevision and planning has been that we have spent public funds more lavishly for relief purposes than has any other country. Since 1933 we have been driving toward integrated relief administration. We have tried out many plans and have operated them simultaneously, but at the opening of the year 1937 we had not yet developed an integrated national plan for relief. There seems to be little doubt among responsible citizens that a permanent plan of relief administration is needed both to handle the continuing problem and to cope with future emergencies. In view of this fact, it is reasonable that a plan for the study of the social aspects of relief policies should be formulated and carried out. It is the purpose of this monograph to propose this kind of plan for research.[1]

---

[1] Closely related to the present monograph and necessarily overlapping to some extent is the bulletin by Chapin, F. Stuart, and Queen, Stuart A. *Research Memorandum on Social Work in the Depression.* (monograph in this series) It deals primarily with social work other than relief, and should be consulted in connection with numerous problems raised here.

A seemingly infinite number of special questions can be asked about the social effects of relief policies, but it was believed better to state a few major problems and to suggest the ramifications which these major problems have. Twelve such problems have been described briefly below. They are not of equal importance, but it is believed that together they suggest a plan of research which would provide answers to some theoretical questions and many practical questions, and would put us in a position to profit by our experience in the formulation of permanent relief policies. The problems outlined deal in some measure with administrative issues, but for the most part they point toward a consideration of the end results of relief policies which have guided administration. In effect the statements of the projects for research ask two questions:

(1) What have been the social effects of relief policies during the depression?

(2) Are these the social effects which we should like to have result from relief policies in the future?

The second question, involving values, is of course not in itself a scientific question. But its answer is the goal toward which study of the first question leads us.

The specific questions which have been asked about each of the twelve problems are illustrative rather than exhaustive. Any competent social worker or research worker who is interested in one of the problems can think of other questions to ask, some of which could doubtless become the basis for a large research project. Our aim has been to emphasize the need for a comprehensive study of the social effects of relief policies. Many brief, special studies have been made, but they do not provide an adequate basis for proposals for the reconstruction of relief policies or for proving the soundness of those which we had had. Systematic plans of research are needed for this purpose.

It is hoped that the publication of this monograph may enlist the interest of research workers in this field throughout the country in cooperative studies of the social effects of relief policies. Despite the fact that since May, 1933, there has been a federal relief administration assisting in the formulation and administration of relief policies, there has been much variety in local relief policies, and the effects of the same policy have been different in various geographical areas. A single large-scale study of the problems outlined below in one state or a group of contiguous states would not be satisfactory; studies should be made of the same problem in all of the major geographical divisions of the country. Variations in results will be found, and the reasons for these variations should be determined, because they will be of fundamental importance in the re-formulation of federal and state relief policies. In practice, the local adaptations of a general relief policy have been made hastily, and it is to be suspected that the personal interests and ability of the administrator counted for more than any actual differences in social conditions. We have experimented. Under the circumstances that has been inevitable and probably desirable. Now that these experiments have been going on for seven years it is time to audit the books and see what kind of social balance sheet we can produce.

From the beginning the Federal Emergency Relief Administration has maintained a Division of Research as an aid to effective administration. In spite of the fact that the Division has had to do its work at greater speed than was desirable, it has illustrated again the relation of continuous research to good social welfare administration, a fact which hitherto too few social workers have been willing to admit. Through their schools of social work and social science departments the universities have for a number of years been placing more and more emphasis upon "research and statistics" in social welfare administration. It is hoped that this monograph may be in line with this developing interest and become the basis for an extensive attack upon the research problems connected with relief policies.

1. THE FRAMEWORK OF RELIEF POLICIES

Relief policies may be classified under three general types: direct relief, work relief, and relief aspects of public works. There will be some objection to the classification of public works as a form of relief, but a considerable part of the expansion of public works during the depression can have no other explanation. Public works projects were substitutes for either direct relief or work relief in a considerable proportion of the cases. A comprehensive study of the social effects of relief policies will of necessity take into consideration the policies of the three types of governmental agencies.

1. Direct Relief. Policies concerning direct relief have three types of variations: temporal, geographical and hierarchical. Between 1929 and 1936 many changes in relief policies occurred. A complete study of relief in a county or a state during the depression would have to take into consideration the shifts of policies which occurred from time to time, and the overlapping of policies during some periods. For convenience in this monograph the period prior to May, 1933, when the Federal Emergency Relief Act was passed, is called the *pre-federal* period. This is not strictly accurate, because the Reconstruction Finance Corporation extended loans to local governmental units for relief purposes in 1932, and in the early part of 1933, before the establishment of the FERA, it began advancing to the states money which, it was understood, would not be repaid to the federal government. We have referred to the period from May, 1933, until November, 1935 (the approximate date on which the FERA was liquidated), as the *federal* period. This period includes the CWA work program and the FERA work program as well as federal aid for direct relief. The third period in direct relief policies runs from November, 1935, to the present, and for convenience has been called the *post-federal* period. These three periods suggest the three major temporal variations in policies. It should not be assumed, however, that there was no continuity in relief policies. As a matter of fact, policies which had been developed in New York and New Jersey during the pre-federal period influenced greatly the policies of the federal government.

Geographical variations in relief policies are probably more numerous than *temporal* variations. In the pre-federal period each state law relating to poor relief probably varied in some degree from every other state law, although there was a general similarity among all of these laws because of their derivation from the old English poor law. The local governmental units responsible for relief were counties, towns, townships, and cities, and in the same state numerous variations in policies existed simultaneously. There were some important differences in policies governing the administration of relief in areas prevailingly rural or prevailingly urban.

One must keep always in mind the *hierarchical* variations, by which we refer to the changes which occurred in the statement or interpretation of relief policies when they were handed down from a higher to a lower unit of government. The FERA transmitted regulations to the states. It would be surprising if, in the case of any single regulation handed down by the federal administration to the states, all of the forty-eight state administrations accepted it in the same terms or understood it to mean the same thing. The regulation was transmitted again by each state administration to its branch offices or to the local governmental units administering relief. A policy, then, which passed down the whole range of the governmental hierarchy to the family on relief usually underwent some change and often serious change. In some instances it is probable that a relief policy which was started on its journey from the FERA never actually reached the client; it was eliminated by agreement before it reached him. Consequently, the study of the "social aspects of relief policies" in a given state or locality requires that the actual, as well as the official, federal policies be determined and considered.

2. Work Relief. Work relief policies show the same kinds of variation as direct relief policies: temporal, geographical and hierarchical. Local work relief programs were in existence on a small scale as early as 1930, and state relief administrations with minor works programs began to appear in 1931, of which that of New York State is perhaps the best known. Four work relief periods can be distinguished: the pre-federal period, the CWA period, the FERA period and the WPA period. These periods are quite distinct; both the statutes and the rules and regulations separate one from the other. In the pre-federal period the geographical variations in work relief policies were many and sharp; they were all experimental, and there were many laboratories between 1929 and 1933. There were some similarities among the work relief programs of localities or states in any one of the major regions of the country, but the similarities were probably less than in the case of direct relief. Under the CWA variations continued to exist but tended to represent state types. The federal government gradually established more uniformity of policies during the FERA period, but it was not until the WPA period that the work program acquired some approximation to a national plan with uniform policies operative in all states. However, too much cannot be assumed regarding the similarity of the policies governing the operation of projects. Some local adaptations to special conditions occurred, and it is probable that variations occurred because of the influence of an administrator or other persons in positions of power—this kind of variation may be more nearly hierarchical than geographical. Wage scales and maximum budgets varied among the geographical regions and between urban and rural areas. Undoubtedly many changes in federal policies occurred during their transmission through the governmental hierarchy. Statements of policy were misunderstood or were deliberately altered without notice to the federal administration. Changes in minor details of policies are perhaps of little consequence, but the federal rules and regulations were sometimes stated in rather general terms which made it necessary for the state administrator to interpret them for state use, and these interpretations introduced considerable variety into even the WPA program.

3. Relief Aspects of Public Works. Policies governing public works probably received more formal and rigid statement than other relief policies. This lack of flexibility accounts somewhat for the slower action of the agencies responsible for public works. But every highway or housing project was not operated alike; adaptations of policy were made for a variety of reasons. Public works had been used as a relief measure to a decreasing extent by the states and localities and to an increasing extent by the federal government prior to May, 1933, but the programs were limited. Under the federal program public works projects were authorized and supervised by a number of federal agencies, the most important of which were the Public Works Administration and the Departments of War and the Navy. Funds were made available to each of these agencies for what ordinarily would be called public works. Most of the projects were sublet to contractors, yet it was the aim of these agencies not only to get important construction work done, but also to provide employment at customary wages to a large number of unemployed persons, and some of these unemployed persons were taken from relief rolls. To whatever extent employees on public works projects were taken deliberately from relief rolls this part of the program should be considered as a relief measure. The public works policies underwent temporal changes, but they were governed less by geographical differences than by the special characteristics of each project. All of these projects were directly or indirectly under the supervision of federal officials; thus hierarchical variations were practically eliminated.

Sources of information regarding the characteristics of relief policies may be regarded as primary and secondary. The primary sources may be divided into five classes: (1) federal statutes, orders, rules, regulations, letters and telegrams; (2)

state statutes, orders, rules, regulations, letters, telegrams and minutes of staff or board meetings; (3) local ordinances, rules, regulations and minutes of staff or board meetings; (4) instructions, rules, regulations and minutes of staff or board meetings of private relief agencies; (5) unofficial sources such as personal recollections, newspaper items, etc. There are many secondary sources, but the following are the most important: (1) *Chronology of the Federal Emergency Relief Administration,* issued by the Works Progress Administration, 1937; (2) state manuals, books of procedure and policy books; (3) local manuals, books of procedure and policy books; (4) library collections of public documents; (5) Congressional Hearings; and (6) the files of the Charity Organization Department of the Russell Sage Foundation. The first step in the study of any of the problems outlined below would be to define the relief policies involved, and it might be necessary to consult several different sources for this purpose.

2. SOURCES OF DATA

The principal sources of data for the study of the social effects of relief policies are not numerous, but those indicated here do not exhaust the list. However, it is believed that they are the most important sources. They are classified as primary and secondary sources as follows in alphabetical order:

(1) Primary sources:
   a. Accounting records.
   b. Applications, requests and referral notations in public employment offices.
   c. Case records.
   d. Contractors' project records.
   e. Factory employment and production records.
   f. Federal, state and local files for general administration.
   g. Hospital and clinic records.

  h. Legislative acts.
  i. New data from clients and other persons by means of surveys.
  j. Office records of private physicians.
  k. Personnel files of relief agencies.
  l. Project applications and work records.
  m. Records of contributions to and expenditures of private relief agencies.
  n. Records of marriage license offices.
  o. Registry of vital statistics.
  p. State and local files of complaints.
  q. Newspaper files.
  r. Personal recollections.
(2) Secondary sources:
  a. Auditors' reports.
  b. Publications of nonrelief governmental agencies.
  c. Publications of private research organizations.
  d. Published reports of federal, state and local relief agencies.
  e. Reports of social service directors and field representatives.
  f. Unpublished summaries of data in federal, state and local relief offices.

Many of the financial records will be on file in federal offices in Washington: that is, those original records which were necessary for control by the federal administration. In some states case records will be on file in the offices of the local relief administration, but in others, where there has been a strong state relief organization, the case records will have been assembled in a central place. In at least one state all of the records, except those lent to the local agencies in the post-federal period, have been put into a library and catalogued for research or reference purposes; this may have been done in some other states, but, if so, it is not known to the writers. The second step for the research worker, after he has defined the relief policies in force, will be to locate the sources for his study. A number of the projects suggested below may require new data which will have to be secured by schedule or questionnaire directly from former clients and other persons. After exploratory analysis of the projected study it will often be found that certain important data were not included in the case records or other records. Securing the new data will be attended by difficulties, but in many cases it doubtless can be done.

3. NOTE ON METHOD

Some of the studies suggested in the following chapters will be quantitative and some of them will be non-quantitative. Certain subjects may lend themselves to both methods. While an effort has been made, in so far as possible, to suggest projects which lend themselves to statistical analysis, many important problems require other types of analysis. For example, the definition of certain policies will require case studies, and light may be thrown upon both policies and practices by autobiographical studies by persons who have been closely connected with the administration of relief for all or a large part of the depression period. If important questions which may be asked about the social effects of relief policies are to be answered, some of the answers will have to be sought from nonstatistical studies. This caution is suggested, because the projects which the writers have outlined may seem to lean heavily upon statistical research.

Some of the projects for research have many subdivisions. It is believed that this will facilitate a wider participation in this large decentralized plan for research on the part of universities and other research agencies. The form in which many of the research problems are proposed is not intended as final. Some research workers will want to restate certain of the problems presented. There is room for many contributions to a better understanding of the problems involved in the administration of relief.

The "effects" of relief policies are very complex, and the causes of the effects may be even more complex. It will be difficult to define exactly the effects in some problem situations; it will be impossible to identify all of the effects. Whenever a subdivision of one of the projects is to be studied, careful qualitative analysis will have to precede the collection of data, and terms will have to be defined. Causes of effects may involve psychological, sociological, economic, political and administrative factors. Few of the problems outlined in the following chapters fall exclusively in the field of a single social science; they cannot be parcelled out to the various academic departments. The research worker who undertakes to study any one of the problems indicated as a subdivision of a project will have to be prepared to consider all of the aspects of the problem.

4. ORGANIZATION FOR RESEARCH

A brief statement regarding the organization for research which exists or may exist for the study of the problems described below is in order. A cursory examination of the projects outlined will be sufficient to convince the reader that a comprehensive study of the social effects of relief policies will be expensive. Nevertheless, it is believed that the interest of universities and research agencies in the problems of relief is sufficient to assure some relatively large and many small research projects being undertaken. It is the hope of the Committee for the Study of Social Aspects of the Depression that many university professors and their advanced students will undertake studies suggested by this monograph. Certain existing research organizations have in the past done some work in this general field. Among them may be mentioned the Brookings Institution, the National Bureau of Economic Research, the National Industrial Conference Board, the Russell Sage Foundation, and the Twentieth Century Fund. It is reasonable to assume that one or more of these organizations may be interested in pursuing such studies further, and the encouragement which universities have given to their social science departments and their schools of social work in the past gives hope that they may make important contributions during the next few years to a better understanding of the problems of relief administration.

It will occur to many that the plans of research here presented might properly be undertaken by a special committee which would cover the entire field. There is something to be said for this procedure, but it should be emphasized that the cost would be staggeringly large. It would be so large that the writers have been unwilling to put down a figure which they could defend as a reasonable estimate. If ample funds should become available, however, an organization for a centrally controlled study of the social effects of relief policies could be set up.

Under any circumstances a small continuing co-ordinating committee should be set up. It could do a great deal toward bringing together, after a few years, the studies which will have been made and compiling the results of research for publication in a separate volume or volumes. Some such plan is needed, if we are to profit most by the rather tumultuous experience which we have had since 1929 with relief administration. This co-ordinating committee would have to have a budget and a small staff to carry on its work, but it would not be an expensive undertaking.

Chapter II

Degree of Destitution Required for Granting Relief

HOW "needy" must an individual or family have been in order to be granted relief? Must they need food for the next meal? Must they have missed a few meals in the recent past? Must they be out of fuel? Must they lack sufficient clothes to keep them warm? Must they live in a house which leaks or needs painting or which needs other repairs? What was the standard of destitution which the relief agency used? In different times and places and among different agencies there were, of course, many standards of destitution upon which were based decisions to grant relief, but in any case, even in the most inefficiently organized agency, there was an acknowledged standard below which it was not necessary for a family to sink in order to obtain relief.

1. POLICIES

In Rules and Regulations No. 3 of the Federal Emergency Relief Administration, issued July 11, 1933, the position is taken that it is obligatory upon any agency receiving federal funds to see that the needy receive "sufficient relief to prevent physical suffering and to maintain minimum living standards." It was further said, to summarize, that the amount of relief (whether relief is the sole means of subsistence or supplementary to some small income) must be based upon an estimate of the weekly needs of the individual or family. This conception of minimum subsistence, issued as an FERA order, represents the adoption of a concept, to be applied in all parts of the country, similar to that held by the best private and local public agencies. Was this statement of policy a means of establishing a standard of minimum subsistence throughout the country? If not, then how did it affect the standard of subsistence in various states and localities?[1]

For many years the phrase, "the American standard of living," has been used rather loosely. It meant something different to every person who used it, and it was a concept without much tangible content. The experience with relief and the effort of the FERA to define minimum subsistence objectively for administrative purposes may have given us a bottom for the concept known as the "American standard of living." Whatever may be the permanent effects of the experience with this particular relief policy, stated by the FERA for the first time as a national policy, the problem deserves a thorough analysis. If definite content has been given to the concept of minimum subsistence, even in a few localities and states, then future consideration of relief, either general or categorical, has a starting point.

Data for the study of this problem are abundant. The degree of destitution had to be determined after the application had been received before relief was granted, in order, first, to decide whether or not relief would be given, and second, to determine the amount of relief required to provide the minimum standard of subsistence. Consequently the case records give an account of the family economic status as the legal justification for granting relief. Under rules and regulations a family budget had to be made, and this became a part of the case record. This budget was probably an approximation to the theoretical state or municipal budget prepared as a guide for the relief staff. The theoretical budget was usually made by competent home economists

---

[1] The relief policies of the Rural Rehabilitation Agency and the Resettlement Administration varied in some respects from the general policies. A thorough study of the social effects of the relief policies of these agencies should be made.

who were familiar with studies of this problem. All of this information is available in the case records and in the files of the home economists.[2]

2. RESEARCH PROBLEMS

A few questions may be stated in order to point the problem more clearly:

1. What criteria were used for the determination of the degree of destitution of a farm family?
    (1) Was insufficient food the principal consideration?
    (2) Did the condition of the house enter into the final decision?
    (3) Under what circumstances would fuel and clothing be important?
    (4) Was health or the need of medical attention a factor?
    (5) Did lack of seeds or farm tools and machinery affect the decision?
2. What criteria were used for the determination of the degree of destitution of an urban family?
    (1) Was need of food the first consideration?
    (2) Did inability to pay rent become decisive in some cases?
    (3) How important were matters of health?
    (4) Did the condition of the house or apartment affect the final decision?
3. Did the specific family budget differ markedly from the state or municipal theoretical budget?
    (1) As to the amount of the food allowance?
    (2) As to the amount of the clothing allowance?

---

[2] The significance of the problem of the minimum budget for evaluating health in the depression is discussed at length in Collins, Selwyn D., and Tibbitts, Clark. *Research Memorandum on Social Aspects of Health in the Depression.* (monograph in this series)

(3) As to the amount of the fuel allowance?

(4) As to the amount of the rent allowance?

(5) As to the amount allowed for miscellaneous items?

(6) Compare the percentage deviations from the theoretical budget in different states and different localities in the same state.

(7) Compare the percentage deviations in minority groups.

(8) Consider the budgeting of income of older children in order to determine the amount of relief.

4. How much improvement occurred in the standard of subsistence after relief was given?

(1) How much more adequate was the food?

(2) Was the housing condition improved?

(3) Was fuel more adequate?

(4) Was clothing furnished in adequate quantities?

(5) Was medical attention provided? Did health of members of the family improve?

5. Is it possible to determine the point in a family's standard of living at which destitution becomes dangerous to health and morale?

(1) Among the applicants for relief, how often does insufficient food appear as the most important factor?

(2) How often do housing conditions appear to be sufficient as a basis of action by the relief agency?

(3) Is lack of clothing a primary consideration in an important number of cases?

(4) Could a weighted index of the various factors in family destitution be constructed?

6. What differences appear in standard of living and costs of administration, when relief is provided:

(1) Through a commissary?

(2) By orders to stores?

(3) By cash?

3. AN ILLUSTRATION OF METHOD

The answers to these questions can be obtained in some localities, if not for a whole state or the country. There is perhaps no problem in this report for the study of which more adequate statistical material exists than for this one. Some limited studies of certain of these questions have been made, and the method of approach may be illustrated by Harriet Morgan's "A Study of the Food Purchased by or Supplied to 1,729 Relief Families in Rockford, Illinois, March, 1934." This study was done under the auspices of the Elizabeth McCormick Memorial Fund. Miss Morgan says:

"All families on full food relief whose itemized sales slips for the month of March could be obtained from the stores selected were included in the study. A total of 1,729 families— 29 per cent of the March active case load—was studied. The families studied are believed to be fairly representative of Rockford relief families."

Explaining the collection of data, she says:

"Data regarding the families' food purchases were obtained from the duplicate sales slips. All food items recorded on the duplicate sales slips, which represented one month's food purchases of a family, were copied. Non-food articles such as soap, blueing and starch, recorded on the sales slips, were disregarded. Data regarding the family composition, the monetary value of the month's grocery purchase orders, the additional fresh milk allowance, and the kinds and quantities of surplus food commodities received by the families during the period of the study were obtained from records in the county relief office and the surplus food depot."

The purchases of various kinds of foods were compared for persons by age and sex, and compared with a theoretical food budget. Of the list of families studied 327 did not receive surplus foods, whereas 1,402 families did get this additional food; the two groups are analyzed separately. The "average amount purchased" of any food item is compared with the "standard for adequate diet," and the percentage of adequacy is shown; this information is presented by size of families, and then in another table appear the mode, median, mean and standard deviation of the amount of food and coffee purchased by various sized family groups. From this analysis the kind and amount of specific deficiencies were determined for the "surplus food" group and for the "non-surplus food" group, a comparison of which indicates little difference in the kinds of deficiency. Miss Morgan's study has a somewhat different purpose from the project here proposed: she was interested in what food was purchased after relief was awarded, whereas it is here proposed to study an earlier stage of the relief process in order to determine the criteria for admission to relief status. Similar data, but in greater variety, will be required, but the immediate objective of the analysis will be different. Whereas Miss Morgan was really studying the judgments of clients, it is here proposed to study the standard of values used by relief workers.

Chapter III

Social Effects of Relief Policies upon the Family as a Social Group[1]

I T IS A reasonable assumption that the distribution of relief on such a scale as was necessary during the depression would have some important effects upon the family as a social group. It is not so clear, however, that these effects have initiated new permanent directions of change in either the structure or the functions of the family. The effects of relief policies may have produced only temporary adaptations within the family group.

1. POLICIES

These are problems for research, but the policy-making authority and the sources of data will differ considerably from those available for the study of other projects outlined herein. For the most part the relief policies which have affected the family as a social group are state and local policies. Federal transient policies may have been a factor, but with this exception the policies promulgated by the FERA probably have had little direct effect upon the family as a social group. This proposition does not contradict the general purpose of all relief, which was to enable individuals, who generally lived in families, to survive and preserve their health, because relief was available for any individual who needed it regardless of his family status. Policies regarding transients, however, may have been related to

---

[1] For more detailed proposals for research on the effects of the depression on the family see Stouffer, Samuel A., and Lazarsfeld, Paul F. *Research Memorandum on the Family in the Depression.* (monograph in this series)

19

desertion and, hence, to the disintegration of family life. Case records as sources of data are relatively more important for the study of these problems than they are for the study of most of the other projects.

The determination of exactly what these policies were will differ considerably from the usual procedure, because the policies which affected the family as a social group were state and local policies, which were not issued as rules and regulations were generally issued. They were communicated mainly by word of mouth and rarely by ordinary modes of publication. They originated in staff conferences or in committee meetings and were taken by consent. In fact, they were probably regarded as matters of case work technique rather than policies. Occasional references to an agreement regarding some point of policy which might affect the family as a group may be found in minutes of staff or committee meetings, but for the most part policies will have to be inferred from case records. Therefore, this project contemplates what is essentially a study of the social effects of social case work as it was practiced by the state and local relief administrations.

2. PROBLEMS

One of the problems requiring investigation is the social effects of relief policies upon marriage. Marriage statistics during the depression show that the marriage rate declined until some time in 1933 when it started to rise. But these statistics reflect the general marriage rate; they do not permit an analysis of marriage rates among relief and work relief families. In the pre-federal period case records in most localities may have little information about marriage, but the problem is mainly one of determining a marriage in a family. If a sufficiently large sample of names and addresses with other pertinent data were taken from the official registry of marriages, these names could be traced through the relief rolls and marriages among relief families in this period ascertained. During the federal period all well-organized local relief agencies—there were some in every state—will have case records reasonably adequate for the study of the problem. The writers were told by relief workers in eight different states that marriage in a family would be noted in the case record, because this fact influenced the amount of the budget allowance for the family. There seems to be, then, no doubt that marriage rates by nationality, occupation and the stage in the relief experience can be determined for relief families.

But the effect which relief policies had on this rate is more difficult to ascertain with any degree of reliability. Outside of a few states it is probable that in the pre-federal period the relief workers knew little about marriages in their families, even though in a general way they may have been concerned about it; but in the federal period a better quality of social case work was brought into the administration of relief. This carried over into the post-federal period of direct relief. There was a conscious effort on the part of relief workers in some agencies to discourage marriage among their clients, but on the other hand some of the private agencies bought marriage licenses occasionally for young people who wanted to marry, although one or both families might be receiving relief at the time. In the case records of the better public agencies notation was made, when the worker learned that a marriage was being planned in one of the relief families, and a further notation was made of the worker's advice or action. It appears that many young people postponed marriage and that the advice of the worker may have had something to do with the postponement, but some relief workers believe that eventually the young people tended to marry in spite of the relief situation. The postponement may have been longer in the case of skilled or white collar workers than it was among families of unskilled workers. In some localities it seems to have been the policy to require the newlyweds to live with either the husband's family or the wife's family; this is believed to have delayed many marriages. But the boy sometimes became a transient in order to establish an independent relief status and then married. One interesting part of this study would be to determine the amount of time elapsing between marriage and the application for relief as a new family unit. As the depression dragged on, the old stigma attached to relief tended to disappear because so many millions were on relief. This fact, coupled with the further fact that the relief allowance was based upon the needs of the individual in the circumstances in which he found himself, especially after the spring of 1933, may have made marriage easy, because young people could see no difference between receiving relief together after marriage and living on relief in their respective families before marriage. A study of a large number of case records to determine the effects of relief policies upon marriage would undoubtedly reveal other important facts than those mentioned above, but these are suggestive.

Another problem for research is the relation of relief status to the birth rate. This question is at least as old as Malthus, and it would seem that the experience with relief during this depression offers a controlled experiment which should provide a reliable contemporary answer to it.[2] The time factor is particularly important in the study of the birth rate among relief families: it must be correlated with at least two other important factors, namely, the length of time on relief and the kind of relief being given at the time of conception. The reliability of the answer will also be conditioned by nationality and racial factors, which should be held constant. In connection with the determination of refined birth rates there are a number of related special problems. It is a common opinion among obstetricians that the number of abortions, both spontaneous and induced, has increased during the depression. Statistics of abortions are

---

[2] See Stouffer and Lazarsfeld. *Op. cit.* Chapter V

notoriously unreliable; about the only approximate check on the relative number of abortions is the increase or decrease in the number of postabortion cases appearing in clinics and the offices of physicians. If abortions have increased, this might be one fact accounting for a reduced live birth rate only if the number of conceptions did not increase. Since we cannot tell what the trend in conceptions has been it is extremely difficult to relate a possibly increased number of abortions to a decreasing birth rate.

Several social considerations may help to explain the birth rates among relief families: among these would be a decrease in the marriage rate and increases in the number of separations, desertions and divorces. It is the opinion of some relief workers that separations, desertions and divorces among relief families declined. If that were true in the early years of the depresssion, what happened, for instance, during the CWA period, or in 1935 and 1936 when employment in private industry began to rise sharply? The number of stillbirths, which are conventionally excluded in computing the birth rate, may, nevertheless, affect it. There is some opinion to the effect that stillbirths are related to diet and to the state of mind of the mother. During the depression families on relief often had far from either an adequate diet or a balanced diet, and many of them on relief for the first time suffered severe emotional reactions. Another factor having a bearing upon the explanation of the birth rate in relief families is contraception. Few public relief agencies had a definite policy of referring clients to physicians or birth control clinics for contraceptive information and supplies, but these facilities did exist in many cities, and relief workers referred some clients directly but many more indirectly. There has been rather general dissemination of birth control information, and an established clinic is soon heard of in the community. It would be highly desirable to make an extensive study of the effects of unwritten relief policies regarding the referral of clients to private physicians and birth control clinics—in one southern city there is a publicly maintained birth control clinic for Negroes, and many Negro clients were referred to it.

The study of birth rates is one of the more discrete problems for research which is connected with relief policies. There are official records and case records in abundance. Some of the related problems, such as abortions, are difficult, however.

Another question suggested by the birth-rate problem is that of the effect of the amount of relief upon the attitude of the client toward the cost of a new baby. Relief budgets were determined on the basis of the number in the family and the age and sex distribution of members of the family. If pregnancy occurred, especially during the federal period, the mother might get some special items of diet and be referred often to a prenatal clinic. After the baby was born, allowances of milk, cod-liver oil and other things were often made. In some localities the physicians believe that the average relief client received more adequate medical care while on relief than ever before. After the CWA period the work relief client was given an amount of work sufficient to earn wages equal to the requirements of his budget. An addition to the family simply meant that the wage earner would have a few more hours' work each week, and, consequently, there was not so much reason for regarding the birth of another baby as a calamity. Under any circumstances the "why" of conception among relief families involved is complex: such things as the client's attitude toward his responsibility for members of his family, or his idea of a suitable standard of living and his knowledge of contraception require consideration. In some of the larger cities where reasonably good case work was done the records will throw some light on this subject, but the possibility of quantitative analysis of the problem is limited.

It would not be surprising to find that infant mortality among relief families was relatively high, but no comprehensive effort has been made to determine it. The undernourishment or mal-nutrition of the mother during pregnancy is believed in some cases to have some effect upon the developing foetus, and it is well known that the diet of the baby after birth may be a deter-mining factor in its survival. Breast-fed babies may suffer be-cause of deficiencies in the mother's milk, and bottle-fed babies may suffer either for lack of sufficient food or because of defi-cient elements in the diet. It would not be surprising to find that food baskets lacked certain important elements of diet or that allowances of cash or grocery orders were inadequate to provide the necessary diet for infants. A thoroughgoing study of infant mortality among relief families is likely to be baffling, because conclusions will have to be based not only upon the determined rates of mortality but also upon an analysis of the content of food orders. Case records in some localities will have no informa-tion about diets, but it is probable that there were enough well-operated agencies which have such records to make a useful study of the problem. The validity of the results found from such a study will depend partly upon statistical analysis and partly upon the reasoned judgment of competent investigators.

Relief policies may have affected divorce rates in various ways. It is common knowledge that divorce rates go down during a severe economic depression, but we have little more knowledge of divorce among relief families than that derived from casual acquaintance with case records. It would be interesting to know how the divorce rate among relief families compares with both the general divorce rate and the divorce rate among families of low economic status. But there are other questions which may be asked about divorce among relief families. Some relief agen-cies, probably in most cases private agencies, have helped a client to obtain a divorce by advancing the court costs or by securing free legal assistance from the local legal aid society. It has long been the practice of private agencies to attempt to force the pay-ment of alimony or support to their clients, where the offending individual had evaded it, and public agencies have occasionally taken such cases into court. During the depression the case loads were so heavy that it is probable that not much of this was done, although it is one of the traditional "resources" used by social agencies. A study of the experience of both public and private relief agencies with efforts to assure the payment of alimony and support would be worth undertaking. Any study of aspects of divorce among relief families should be accompanied by due consideration of the previous economic status of the parties to the suit. It is almost certain that case records everywhere will have notations of divorces which have occurred during the time the families were getting relief, because, again, the divorce affects the budget allowance and would have to be recorded. The records of the state department which compiles divorce statistics would be an important source of data.

Desertion has often been called the "poor man's divorce." The nature and importance of this problem are not well known. Brief reports in years past have been made by individuals connected with particular social agencies, generally private agencies, but there seems to have been no study of the subject during the depression which would give a reliable picture of it. Some relief workers believe that some deserters came home, as employment became more and more difficult to find, and they believe that there was a good deal of temporary desertion, some of which involved connivance of the family group. Much speculation is involved in any attempt to give probable explanations of desertion among relief families, but some of it was undoubtedly for prudential reasons: the man thought his family would fare better with him away, because the relief worker would feel a special responsibility for the deserted family; the mother or a son or daughter might be able to get more work on a relief project; the neighbors would sympathize and supplement the aid given by the relief agency; the family might live better, because the man could occasionally send home money from earnings to supplement relief. If there was an increase in the short-time or long-time desertion rates, these prudential considerations may help to explain them.

Some study should be given to the efforts made by relief agencies to re-unite separated couples; wherever such an effort was made, some notation was almost certainly made in the case record. Relief workers believe that there was a good deal of intermittent desertion: some men deserted several times for short periods, which might be accounted for as due to neurotic conditions, irritation in the home situation or periodic search for work. In the early part of the depression the laws of legal settlement in many states prevented the granting of relief to a deserter, the result of which may have been to find the desertion rate declining. But the federal transient program removed some of the problems of the deserter: he could change his name and remain a considerable time in a transient shelter before the staff could discover that he had falsified his record; and, if he were discharged, he could go to another shelter and repeat the process. Relief workers, however, do not think the number doing this was large. Desertion rates may vary in different localities or in different parts of a large city, and they undoubtedly vary according to nationality or race; it will be difficult to determine desertion rates among Negroes, especially in the South, because so many of them were never formally married, and a matriarchal attitude is common among them. What information is available in regard to frequency and duration of desertion will ordinarily be found in case records after the beginning of the federal period, though not so often in the pre-federal period.

A question which will be difficult to answer but which has considerable social significance is the degree of responsibility which near relatives assumed for a family which had to be supported by other means than its own. The responsibility of relatives of different degrees of consanguinity to assist a dependent kinsman is specified in the poor laws, and relatives have been regarded as one of the primary "resources" used by private relief agencies. In the early years of the depression, when the amount of relief given by public agencies was meager and the service for the most part very inefficient, it is probable that aid from relatives ran into many millions of dollars. It may not be possible to make even a good guess at the amount of such aid which was given before the family asked for relief. After the application was made to a private agency for relief, the case record is likely to contain some information about the amount and kind of assistance given by relatives, and this would also be true of some public agencies, especially after the beginning of the federal period, but the old local public agency learned very little about relatives and recorded less. The use of relatives as a "resource" is characteristic of those private relief agencies which maintain good standards of social case work; it is hardly reflected at all in the records of agencies which either knew nothing about case-work methods or were so overloaded that case work was impossible. Considering the difficulty likely to be encountered in getting statistics of aid provided by relatives, it is probable that a study of this problem will be in the nature of depictive history which might, nevertheless, have much practical value. To know how the relatives assisted and what part the relief worker played in working out plans with them would be decidedly worth knowing.

3. RESEARCH PROBLEMS

Concrete questions regarding the effects of relief policies upon the family as a social group are indicated below:

1. The effects of relief policies upon marriage:
    (1) What was the marriage rate in relief families?
        a. What was the trend down to the autumn of 1933?
        b. Were there important variations in the CWA, FERA work and WPA periods?
        c. Were there significant differences in rates between

families on direct relief and work relief?

d. How do the rates differ by geographical areas or by census tracts in a city?

e. What relation exists between marriage rates and previous occupation or economic status?

f. What are the specific marriage rates among relief families of different national or racial origins?

g. What is the educational attainment of young people getting married?

h. How is the marriage rate related to the length of time the family has been on relief?

i. Were there noticeable variations in urban and rural communities?

(2) What was the policy of the state or local agency toward intended marriages in relief families?

a. Was it stated in an official document?

b. Was it stated in the records of staff meetings?

c. Was it recorded in the minutes of the meetings of an advisory committee?

d. Was the policy less formal and more like a procedure of case work methods?

e. Did Rural Rehabilitation and Resettlement Administrations aid rural young people to proceed with their marriage plans?

(3) Were marriages postponed because of the relief situation?

a. Was the relief worker active in getting a postponement?

b. Was the attitude of the worker different toward marriages between a client and another person not on relief as compared with the attitude toward a marriage between two clients?

c. Did the amount of the probable relief budget deter young people from getting married?

    d. Was postponement eventually ended by marriage regardless of relief status?

    e. Was the fear of having children a conscious motive for postponing marriage?

    f. Giving due weight to the age distribution of the young people, was the later relative respectability of relief accompanied by a decline in postponed marriages?

    g. What effect did CWA have upon postponed marriages?

(4) Where did the newlyweds live?

    a. In their own newly established homes?

    b. In the homes of the bridegrooms?

    c. In the homes of the brides?

    d. Where there was doubling up of families, was there a significant number of conflict situations arising?

2. Effects of relief policies upon the birth rate in relief families:

(1) What was the birth rate in relief families?

    a. Was there a significant decline down to the autumn of 1933?

    b. Were there significant variations in the CWA, FERA work and WPA periods?

    c. Were there variations according to geographical areas or census tracts?

    d. How was the previous occupation or economic status related to the birth rate?

    e. How does the confinement rate, allowing for exposure to risk of pregnancy, in relief families compare with the confinement rate of nonrelief families of similar religion, nationality and occupational status?

f. Was the birth rate lower after going on relief than for a similar period before going on relief?

g. Did postponement of marriage reduce the birth rate?

(2) Was there an increase in termination of pregnancies before time for confinement?

a. Because of spontaneous abortions?

b. Because of induced abortions?

(3) To what extent was the birth rate reduced by:

a. Separations?

b. Desertions?

c. Divorces?

(4) Was the stillbirth rate high among relief families?

a. Was it related to dietary deficiencies?

b. Was it related to general health problems?

c. Does the rate vary under different relief policies at different times and places?

(5) To what extent did dissemination of contraceptive information reduce the birth rate in relief families?

a. Were birth control clinics established during the depression for the special purpose of serving relief agencies?

b. How many relief families received birth control information at birth control clinics or from private physicians with whom arrangements had been made by relief agencies?

c. Did relief workers refer cases for contraceptive information (both regular relief agencies and nursing agencies)?

3. Effect of relief policies on the attitude toward the cost of new babies:

(1) Was it possible to disregard the cost because:

a. Free maternity care at home or in a hospital was available?

b. Budgets would be readjusted to meet the requirements of a new baby in the family?

c. "Surplus clothing" was available?

d. After work relief became plentiful, father would get additional work?

(2) Did relief families disregard the reduced standard of living which relief necessitated?

    a. Was there a noticeable slowing down of conceptions during the early months of the relief experience?

    b. Did the conception rate rise as families got used to the standard of living imposed by relief status?

    c. Were there significant differences among occupational, ethnic and religious groups?

4. Effects of relief policies upon infant mortality:

(1) What was the infant mortality rate among relief families?

    a. Were there significant variations under different relief-policy periods?

    b. Did ethnic and occupational groups show important variations from their usual rates?

    c. What were the diseases from which death resulted?

    d. Were these specific infant mortality rates different from those obtaining in nonrelief families?

(2) Where infant mortality rates have increased, what were the probable causes?

    a. Can they be attributed to specific dietary deficiencies?

    b. Are there differences in geographical areas and census tracts?

    c. Does infant mortality seem to be related to the conditions of houses in which clients lived?

    d. How important was lowered resistance to disease because of insufficient food?

5. Effects of relief policies upon the divorce rate:
   (1) How was the rate affected?
      a. Did relief agencies pay the court costs?
      b. How many relief clients were assisted by legal aid societies to obtain divorces?
      c. How did the rate in relief families compare with the rate in families of similar previous occupational status?
      d. Did relief workers attempt to adjust family relations in order to prevent divorce?
   (2) What was the attitude of relief agencies toward alimony and child support?
      a. Did they attempt to collect alimony in order to reduce the relief budget?
      b. What efforts were made to obtain support for children?

6. Effects of relief policies upon desertion:
   (1) What was the desertion rate?
      a. Among different occupational groups?
      b. Among those with similar previous economic status?
      c. Among different ethnic groups?
      d. Among different religious groups?
      e. Did the rate vary in geographical areas and census tracts?
      f. Can the rates be compared with desertion rates in a nonrelief control group?
   (2) What inducements to desert did relief policies provide?
      a. Would the investigator feel more than ordinary responsibility for the deserted family?
      b. Would the mother be given more work relief or a better job?
      c. Would the sympathy of the neighbors result in an

improvement in the living conditions of the client?

d. Can it be determined whether or not husbands deserted in order to send home small sums of money to supplement relief allowances?

e. If the husband deserted during the federal transient period, would he live better in a transient shelter than at home?

f. Did relief agencies attempt to bring back deserters?

(3) What was the duration of desertion?

a. Did desertion last until economic circumstances changed?

b. How many deserters were repeaters?

c. In the pre-federal period did the laws of legal settlement tend to shorten the period of desertion?

d. After the beginning of the federal transient program did the average length of desertion increase?

7. Effects of relief policies upon the amount of assistance provided by near relatives:

(1) How much assistance was given by relatives:

a. Before the family asked for relief?

b. After the family began receiving relief?

c. Did the relief worker arrange family conferences regarding relief?

(2) What was the effect upon the support of aged couples or individuals by their children?

a. Did relief agencies allow relief to aged persons living with their children, if the young people were earning an insufficient amount to support all of them?

b. Were self-sustaining young people forced to put out old people to avoid going on relief themselves?

c. If relief was allowed in such a home, did the aged parent or the young person have to apply for it?

      d. How important was this problem?

8. Effects of relief policies upon children in the home:

(1) Did more nearly adequate relief affect the removal of children from the home?

(2) Were there noticeable effects among children of school age in so far as conduct problems were concerned?

(3) Were there noticeable effects upon the health of school children as reflected by physical examinations?

(4) Did adequacy of relief tend to remove pressure upon older children to find employment?

4. AN ILLUSTRATION OF METHOD

The study of such problems as those outlined above presents many technical difficulties, but it is believed that much light can be thrown upon the effects of relief policies upon the family as a social group, if terms are carefully defined and the problem is clearly seen. Several careful studies of limited scope dealing with the birth rate have already been made, and a brief description of one of these may be suggestive for further study of not only the birth rate in relief families but also other problems. Because of the care with which scope and terms have been defined, a study made in Milwaukee in 1934 by Professor Samuel A. Stouffer has been selected for purposes of illustration.[3] This is a study of comparative birth rates among relief and nonrelief families in Milwaukee from October 1, 1930, to December 31, 1933. All families who applied for and received relief, a total of 5,520, were included. A control group of the same number of nonrelief families was used. No confinements were considered in the relief families which occurred sooner than nine months after the family began receiving relief.

---

[3] Stouffer, Samuel A. "Fertility of Families on Relief." *Journal of the American Statistical Association.* 29:295-300. No. 187. September 1934

The procedure for the study, much abbreviated, may be described as follows: The schedule called for the location of the family, the occupation of the husband, the religion of the clergyman who officiated at the wedding, date of death of either spouse, date of separation or divorce, and date and place of birth of each of the children in the family. These schedules were then mailed to both relief and nonrelief families. About 60 per cent replied to the first letter, and an additional 37 per cent responded to the second, third, fourth and fifth letters. All cards were checked against the files of the Milwaukee County Department of Outdoor Relief, and the date of application of relief was recorded—the total duration of relief was not considered. All confinements occurring nine months after relief began and before December 31, 1933, were noted on the card. About 100 cards were discarded because of incomplete data. The cards were coded for occupation as follows: (1) professional and proprietary; (2) clerical; (3) skilled worker; and (4) semiskilled or unskilled worker. There were so few in the first class that they were discarded. Religious affiliation was recorded as Catholic and non-Catholic, determined on the basis of the religion of the officiating clergyman. Twins counted as one confinement and stillbirths the same as live births—each was one confinement. The ratio of births in relief families to births in nonrelief families was then computed.

The results of the study showed that (1) the number of confinements of all subgroups by occupational class and probable religion was greater among relief families, and for all subgroups it amounted to an excess of 35 per cent; (2) the excess of fertility in the relief group is still greater, or 43 per cent, if the calculations are based upon months of exposure to the risk of pregnancy; and (3) the fertility of couples married by a Catholic priest was higher than those not so married, but " 'Catholic' fertility in every *nonrelief* occupational group was lower than that of the 'non-Catholics' in the corresponding *re-lief* occupational group."[4]

Here we have precise definition of a problem and exact statement of results. This study intended to answer one question: What was the differential fertility among relief and nonrelief families in a single city for a specified period? That question was answered. From the standpoint of relief policy, a further pertinent question was not answered, namely, whether or not the differential between the two classes of families, relief and non-relief, would have existed even if there had been no granting of relief.

There are some other problems for study contemplated in No. 2 of the foregoing outline relating to the birth rate in relief families. Relief policies varied in time and space, and there was the major dichotomy of direct relief and work relief. If a national study of birth rates in relation to relief could be undertaken, there would be sufficient cases to answer a larger number of specific questions and perhaps to define more exactly the relation of relief to the birth rate at different times and places.

---

[4] *Op. cit.* P. 300

Chapter IV

Social Effects of Relief Policies upon Health[1]

THAT relief policies affected the health of millions of people requires no abstruse research to demonstrate. These people without income could not pay for medical services themselves; they either suffered for lack of medical attention, which would imply either the absence of, or inadequate medical relief policy, or they received medical attention because of relief policy. Hence, the problem for research is not to discover whether or not there were effects, but to measure the effects. Some study will have to be given to the identification of the kinds of effects in order not to miss important ones, but once they have been identified the problem of determining their extent arises.

1. POLICIES

The effort to organize health services during this depression has been more general, thoroughgoing and sustained than in previous depressions. Medical service in America has been regarded as the concern of the individual to a much larger degree than in most other civilized nations. The medical profession has probably gone further in this country toward making private medicine serve the whole population than in other countries, but the gigantic proportions of dependency brought about by this depression have served to emphasize the inadequacy of private medicine as hitherto practiced and to clarify the need for

---

[1] For a more general consideration of the effects of the depression on health see Collins, Selwyn D. and Tibbitts, Clark. *Research Memorandum on Social Aspects of Health in the Depression*

public medical service which can guarantee adequate attention for those who require medical care. Other nations have long since recognized that the public stake in individual health is a national economic interest of the first importance, namely, the development, restoration and maintenance of working capacity in the individual. The child needs medical attention to assure normal growth to maturity when he should be an able-bodied unit in the working force of the nation; the sick or the injured person requires medical care in order to restore his working capacity or as much of it as possible; the well person should understand the elementary rules of health and hygiene in order to maintain his working capacity. These matters have received more widespread attention from relief agencies during this depression than in any previous depression in this country. This was probably true in the pre-federal period, and it was everywhere noticeable during the federal period.

The problems for research here proposed will be concerned with the effects of administrative policy; they will not have to do with the study of the average health of a sample of the total population, important as that may be, although in some of the proposed research, studies of the average health will of necessity be by-products.

What have been the relief policies regarding the health of clients? How have they been carried out in practice? How much have they affected the health of the recipients of relief? These questions are important for the development of future health relief policies. The answers to them should provide a realistic statement of principles which could guide the development of a national health program, especially for recipients of relief but perhaps for others in the population who are unable to pay the cost of all the medical care which they should have.

In the pre-federal period medical relief policies were as various as state relief laws and municipal ordinances. The large cities had public hospitals and clinics, and there were often many private hospitals and clinics which gave a considerable amount of free service. In rural communities medical relief was less definitely organized; sometimes there were county hospitals, but more often the overseer of the poor appointed one or more physicians who would make home calls or receive patients at his office for which he submitted a bill to the overseer of the poor. After the Federal Emergency Relief Act was passed medical relief became general and somewhat more uniform, although the amounts expended for medical service varied widely even in the same state. On September 10, 1933, the FERA (Rules and Regulations No. 7) issued specific instructions regarding medical relief in the states which received federal money. These instructions covered service by the physician, the dentist and the nurse.

"The physician, dentist and nurse must agree to furnish the same type of service to an indigent person as would be given to a private person; but such service shall be a minimum consistent with good professional judgment and charged for at the agreed rate."

It was further stated that:

"The policy adopted shall be to augment and render more adequate the facilities already existing in the community. . . ."

Medical care was authorized on an individual basis for chronic patients; provision was made for obstetrical care; in general, dental care was to be limited to emergency extractions and repairs. Unusual cases were to receive whatever attention was required. In a memorandum issued July 25, 1933, special plans for transients were promulgated which included provision for medical and health service; these were made more specific by Rules and Regulations No. 8, issued November 6, 1933, which among other things stated:

"It is expected that every transient registered will be given a complete physical examination and that necessary medical care will be provided. . . ."

And February 7, 1935. ". . . further safety and sanitary regulations" for transients were ordered put into effect. The FERA could say little about covering work relief employees by compensation insurance, but in Rules and Regulations No. 3 it is stated that: "Persons employed on work relief projects by the States and their subdivisions ought to be covered by compensation or accident insurance," but such insurance had to be carried by the states. On March 6, 1934, the states were reminded again that under the emergency work relief program responsibility for providing accident compensation insurance rests with the states and localities. Since the Works Progress Administration was a federal agency, accident compensation insurance covering workers on WPA projects was a federal responsibility. Another change occurred when the Resettlement Administration assumed responsibility for relief in certain rural families; the health policies of this agency are not so easily identified. There can be no doubt that it was the intention of the Federal Emergency Relief Administration to provide necessary health and medical service for all members of the relief family.

After the Federal Government withdrew from direct relief in 1935, policies regarding health service were thrown back upon the states, except in so far as WPA workers were concerned. The old relief authorities came into full power again. That they lapsed into their former variety of policies is indicated by the fact that in January, 1936, the township trustees in Indiana, of whom there are 1,016, paid average medical care costs which varied from $.21 to $2.84 per person; that is, the most expensive township had medical relief costs more than thirteen times as high as the township with the lowest per person cost. Thus, it would seem that in so far as medical relief is concerned, there were three periods: pre-federal, federal, and post-federal.

2. PROBLEMS

To make a quantitative appraisal of the social effects of relief policies is the problem for research. Some of it may be accomplished directly, but much of it will have to be approached by indirection. That is the case with health education. The relief agencies did carry on extensive health education; large numbers of clients were exposed to this education either individually or in groups. They were instructed about diets—the amount and kinds of food required for adults and children, for manual workers and brain workers, for sick persons and well persons. Many mothers learned for the first time that cod-liver oil was important as a health protective for the baby, and they heard much about milk in the diet of both adults and children. Simple recipes, with costs indicated, were given to clients in the hope that they would use their meager cash or grocery orders to buy the right kinds of food in the correct quantities. To a limited extent, at least, health education became a regular part of case-work treatment by the social worker. Not only were clients instructed about diets, but they were directed to clinics, perhaps in larger numbers than ever before, in order to be examined or treated for some apparent ailment. Visiting nurses constituted an important adjunct to the relief staff; they not only carried out the treatment orders of the doctor, but they instructed the patient about the care of himself and of other members of the family.

How much effect did this miscellaneous and multifarious health education have? That is the research problem. Copies of grocery orders are probably available in relief records, and recipe leaflets and other dietary material exist in the records of the same agencies. With these two sets of records it may be possible to determine to what extent clients purchased the proper kinds of food. Clinic records will show the number of visits of clients. The record of medical bills paid by the relief agencies should give some clue to the amount of health work done. Visiting nurse associations probably have extensive records of efforts to teach clients how to care for their health. From such material some conception of the amount of health education undertaken can be obtained and perhaps a rough measure of its success.

It would be interesting to know whether or not the relief workers directed clients to clinics, hospitals and doctors in earlier stages of illness than normally occurred. The discovery of symptoms, such as headache, persistent local pain or low fever, may have led to early diagnosis of serious ailments and improved the prognosis or shortened the duration of the illness. The records kept by clinics and doctors contain information which would permit the study of this problem. Dental records are likewise available. In view of the effort being made at the present time by the United States Public Health Service to discover and treat venereal diseases, it would be particularly valuable to investigate the experience of relief agencies with the discovery and treatment of these diseases. In all federal transient shelters and camps clients were examined by a physician, and these records would be a valuable source of data for the study of this particular problem. But the date of diagnosis in relation to the duration of illness should not be restricted to venereal diseases; it is desirable to study these facts with reference to a variety of common ailments.

A number of communicable diseases might easily have become epidemic during the depression, but none at least attained the proportions of the influenza epidemic in 1918. It would be useful to know whether or not the constant vigilance of the relief workers led to early isolation of infected persons and prevented the spread of venereal diseases, tuberculosis, cerebro-spinal meningitis, measles, whooping cough, scarlet fever, mumps and other communicable diseases. This particular study is, of course, only a special phase of the problem of early diagnosis, but it is of sufficient importance to give it separate description.

In some states the relief administration arranged with the medical profession for systematic inoculation of children with toxin-antitoxin. There may be some disagreement within the medical profession as to the wisdom of wholesale inoculation to prevent diphtheria among children, but in some states it did not take this attitude. A study of the incidence of diphtheria in some states, where toxin-antitoxin was given to large numbers of children, and in other states, where no special effort was made to have them inoculated, might throw light on the desirability of requiring inoculation against diphtheria in the same way that vaccination against smallpox is already required in most localities.

Infant and maternal mortality rates have been declining in this country, but public health authorities and social workers have been disturbed because they are so much higher than in some other countries. A special study of mortality among infants and mothers in relief families would be a valuable contribution to the understanding of this problem. These two mortality rates are normally higher among families of a low standard of living than they are among families of comfortable standards. Many thousands of births occurred in families which were receiving relief, including medical relief. Did the supervision of the case worker lead to better prenatal care, more normal deliveries and better postnatal care? How do the mortality rates of infants and mothers in relief families compare with the mortality rates of infants and mothers in the general population or in comparable nonrelief groups? These are questions which can be answered with a reasonable degree of definiteness.

3. RESEARCH PROBLEMS

These problems for research may be outlined as follows:

1. Social effects of health education:
   (1) By what methods and how extensively was instruction regarding the value of cod-liver oil and milk carried on?
       a. Instruction by the case worker?
       b. Instruction by public health nurses?
       c. Distribution of leaflets written in simple language?
       d. Instruction of clients in classes?

(2) How can the effects of health education be measured?
 a. By increased use of milk, when clients were free to use their money or grocery orders as they wished?
 b. By amount of cod-liver oil given to children and by request of clients for a new supply?
 c. By increasing number of voluntary visits to clinics?
 d. By requests of clients for recipes and menus?
 e. By an examination of items on grocery receipts compared with dietary instructions?
 f. An analysis of notations in case records of relief agencies and visiting nurse associations?
2. Stage of illness at which diagnosis was made:
 (1) How often do notations in case records mention symptoms accompanied by statement that client was advised to:
 a. See a physician?
 b. Go to a clinic?
 c. Visit a hospital?
 d. How often did clients act upon the suggestion of the case worker, as indicated by notations in the case records?
 (2) What was done about a diagnosis of venereal disease found among transients?
 a. Was the patient given treatment at a clinic?
 b. Was the patient sent to a hospital for treatment?
 c. Did the attending physician give treatment?
 d. What were the results of treatment?
 (3) At what stage in the development of an illness was diagnosis usually made?
 a. What was the duration of specific illnesses after diagnosis?
 b. How does the duration of a specific illness among clients compare with the usual expected duration?

    c. Can it be determined whether or not diagnosis occurred at a relatively early stage of the illness because of the supervision of the family by a case worker?

3. Experience with communicable disease:
   (1) What do the case records and other records reveal about the occurrence of communicable disease?
     a. What diseases are noted?
     b. At what stage in the development of the disease was it noticed and treatment begun?
     c. Was it possible to protect other members of the family from the disease according to the best known methods of prevention?
   (2) What followed the discovery of such diseases as the following in a relief family or a transient shelter?
     a. Venereal disease?
     b. Tuberculosis?
     c. Cerebro-spinal meningitis?
     d. Measles?
     e. Whooping cough?
     f. Scarlet fever?
     g. Mumps?

4. Results of the wholesale inoculation of children with toxin-antitoxin:
   (1) Was the diphtheria rate low in those states in which the children were inoculated?
   (2) Was the diphtheria rate relatively high in those states which made no systematic effort to inoculate children?

5. Infant and maternal mortality rates:
   (1) What were the infant mortality rates among infants in relief families?
     a. In the first week of life?
     b. By successive months in the first six months of life?
     c. In the first year of life?

      d. In cases of death what were the diagnoses?

      e. How do the rates compare with the similar rates for the general population; with those of a comparable nonrelief group?

      f. How do the causes of death compare with those in the general population; with those of a comparable nonrelief group?

(2) What can be learned about the maternal mortality rate among relief families?

      a. How did it compare with the maternal mortality rate in the general population; with those of a comparable nonrelief group?

      b. What were the prevailing causes of maternal deaths and how do they compare with those in the general maternal population; with those of a comparable nonrelief group?

      c. What part did the relief workers play in the problem of maternal health?

4. AN ILLUSTRATION OF METHOD

A number of small studies of health among clients has been made in various localities, and some more extensive ones have been undertaken. An extensive study of medical-economic problems has been made in California. Although not yet published, it is intended to form the factual basis for presenting a health insurance bill to the legislature. A WPA health project sponsored by the United States Public Health Service has made a sample study of more than 800,000 families to determine the incidence and cost of illness and a special study of about 200,000 families to determine the incidence and cost of communicable disease. Work relief families will be shown in a special tabulation and can be compared with families comparable in other respects but whose incomes are derived from private employment. These studies deal with others than relief clients, but they will shed some light on the health of clients. One of the best collections of health data is in the files of the Medical Bureau of San Francisco; as yet the social and medical data on some 80,000 cases have been analyzed very little.

A study of health by Margaret C. Klem, *Medical Care and Costs in California Families in Relation to Economic Status* (California State Relief Administration), is suggestive to anyone undertaking the study of projects indicated above. "This study presents an analysis of the incidence of illness, the extent and volume of medical care, and the costs of medical care, in relation to family economic status in California, in 1934." The sample selected for this study consisted of 18,527 individuals living in 5,096 families of two or more persons. About 14 per cent of the families were on relief, and about 4 per cent had incomes of $3,000 or more. The families were classified according to economic status, change in economic level and employment status. On the basis of this classification an analysis of the type and kind of medical service received was made for the years 1929 and 1933. It was found that persons on relief had less medical attention than the other groups; the amount of medical attention received increased as income rose. Only 55 per cent of the individuals in relief families had received dental care in the last four years, while of those whose incomes ranged from $1,200 to $3,000 or more approximately 75 per cent had received dental care in the preceding year. This study indicates that in the pre-federal period, at least, medical relief was very inadequate, if we should take the amount of care received by persons with incomes of $1,200 or more as being measurably adequate. It would be interesting to study a similar group of families in the same counties of California during the federal period, and then again in the post-federal period. While Miss Klem's study is concerned in part with problems outside the scope of the projects indicated here, it serves to indicate that objective data can be obtained concerning health matters.

Chapter V

Subjective Effects of Experience with Relief

IT HAS long been known that some clients show neurotic responses to the relief experience and that some of them attempt to work out a permanent adjustment on the neurotic level. During the depression psychiatrists and psychiatric social workers have noticed cases of this kind; much has been written about neurotic symptoms of clients, but there has not been an adequate study of a large number of cases. Neurotic symptoms have a family resemblance, but we do not know under what circumstances during relief experience they begin to appear. Isolated cases have been studied. The neurotic process has been observed and analyzed but usually without specific reference to the impact of the relief experience.[1]

1. PROBLEMS AND POLICIES

During the World War a large number of apparently stable men developed what came to be called "war neuroses." It was observed that these neuroses had their roots in the particular personalities of the individuals but that under ordinary circumstances of stress and strain normal adjustments had been made, whereas under the extraordinary stress and strain of war conditions these individuals developed neurotic adjustments. It seems that an appreciable number of relief clients, who were normally self-maintaining and apparently stable, had "nervous break-

[1] Marcus, Grace. *Some Aspects of Relief in Family Case Work.* New York: Charity Organization Society of New York. 1929. Deals with this problem.

downs" or "went to pieces," that is, developed neurotic symptoms and attempted to make neurotic adjustments during the relief experience. Wherever this occurred, it raised the question of future readjustment in order to restore vocational efficiency, and immediately it complicated relations within the family group. The percentage of such cases in the total relief case load is small, but in the aggregate neurotic cases apparently constitute a large number of individuals and affect seriously many more in the family group.

Obviously the type of research required in a project of this sort is not quantitative but clinical. If a sufficiently large number of cases could be studied, it might be possible to indicate roughly some statistical correlations, but for the most part the study of this problem could at best be expected to result in the description of psycho-social process after points of origin of the neurotic behavior had been established. Such case studies would have therapeutic uses for the psychiatrist and the social worker, but they are not likely to yield definitely quantitative results.

But there were other subjective effects of experience with relief. Neurotic responses are perhaps more easily identified, but changes in the emotional reaction to relief occurred in the non-relief population. As relief policies became more liberal and more people had to accept relief, the stigma was removed, and probably the tension in nonrelief families of low economic status relaxed somewhat when they contemplated the possibility of asking for relief in the future. The community in general came to accept relief more nearly as a right than it had before. This attitude expressed itself in an apparent growing sense of solidarity and the belief that government should make permanent provision for individuals and families who in the future fall victims to the common hazards of life. This new attitude may have accounted to some extent for the huge vote which President Roosevelt received in the election, and it has undoubtedly entered into the creation of a public opinion favorable to social legislation. Verifiable data bearing upon this aspect of the subjective effects of the experience with relief will be difficult to obtain, but a search for a practical method of research would be desirable.

There are several relief policies which touch this problem of neurotic symptoms and personal and family adjustments. In most large relief offices there was an "intake desk," and of course, in all relief offices there were one or more individuals who received applications for relief. It is the judgment of social workers that the first contact with the potential client at the relief office often determines success or failure in case-work treatment; through setting the response pattern to this experience, which almost inevitably has deep implications, a despondent person may be started on the road to constructive readjustment by a skillful case worker at the intake desk, whereas something else happens when the intake desk is occupied by an untrained, tactless person. Many of the large relief agencies place one of their best workers at the intake desk. In the prefederal period, when relief was administered by the local public agencies, the worker at the intake desk was likely to be no more than a clerk, often a political appointee. The intake policy is, therefore, crucial in dealing with the potential neurotic. However, the prevention of emotional maladjustment in the client throughout the relief experience is closely related to the qualifications of the case worker: it is possible for the methods of the case worker to lead either to greater disturbance or to a settling down to a satisfied dependency. Persons who never had to accept relief before their prolonged unemployment during the depression have in many cases developed a feeling of insecurity before asking for relief; the manner in which relief is given may increase this feeling of insecurity and result in more pronounced symptoms of neurosis. Those clients who are particularly sensitive and who prefer work relief to direct relief may develop exaggerated neurotic symptoms because of fear of losing the work relief job. Others may take advantage of the relief situation to realize a long felt desire to be dependent and consequently deteriorate rapidly, unless a skillful case worker observes the symptoms and takes steps to counteract the slide toward a comfortable dependency. Hence, the development of neurotic symptoms during the relief experience is closely bound up with the personnel policies of the relief administration.

The degree of cohesion within the family group is a subject which perhaps lends itself to more specific delineation than some other aspects of emotional maladjustment. The shock of a first relief experience may have been the stimulus which led to transiency of one or more members of the family; under the guidance of a skillful case worker, increased cooperative effort might have given the family greater solidarity. Inadequacy of relief may have caused dissatisfaction and irritation which strained family relations. When such a situation was created, it might have been followed by the breakup of the family or the desertion of one or more members. However, the departure of a member of the family from home did not always indicate estrangement: older boys sometimes did obtain work away from home or went to CCC camps. In the latter case they supplemented family resources, which may have resulted in greater cohesion within the family. A study of selected case records, supplemented by psychoanalytic study, might clarify causes which led to these two opposite responses to the relief experience.

A problem somewhat akin to the one just suggested is the case in which the husband, being completely out of remunerative employment, becomes morose because of his apparent unimportance in the family group, or, accepting the situation without a struggle, settles into a satisfied dependency. Often the wife made application for relief and each week went to the relief office to get the allowance or grocery order. One private agency in Pittsburgh changed its policy regarding the person who should get the relief order and required the husband to come for it so that he would feel that he had some useful place in the family. The wife had to prepare the food and do the usual housework; her activities were not much different from what they had been when the husband was employed, but after losing his job it seemed to him that he had no significant activities. He may not have wanted to go to the relief office, but that did not alter the fact that the family could have got along just as well without him. The private agency referred to above believed that by requiring the husband to be the one to deal with the relief agency, it was forcing him into active participation in the relief experience. The significance of this policy and the importance of its absence in most public agencies can be determined only by an intensive study of records and individuals.

When the WPA began operations, a large number of persons on relief were told that they could not be certified for WPA employment, because they were unemployable. This arbitrary classification must have been quite a shock to many of those who were put into the unemployable group, even though at the time they may have been physically or psychologically unable to work. This dichotomy of relief clients was widely published in the newspapers, and was widely discussed. It had an implication of finality which probably was not intended by the relief administration, but the effect on clients seems to have been to produce either indignation or despondency. Those who were indignant often found work for themselves and refuted their classification, but those who became despondent are less likely to have sought work. What has happened to those who reacted with despondency? Why did they become despondent instead of indignant? Those are questions which should be answered, and approximate answers probably can be obtained through an organized study of case records and the psychoanalytic study of a selected number of individuals.

The emotional consequences of prolonged unemployment and prolonged relief status are not yet clearly understood. These require further study. We know that a considerable percentage of those on relief in the early part of 1936 had been receiving relief for six years. During that period they must have made in many cases a satisfying emotional adjustment to the relief status. They may have long since accepted the condition of poverty as their normal lot and, hence, have become paupers in the real sense of that term. This is an important problem for future relief policy. If the chances of acquiescence to a condition of poverty increase directly with the length of the relief period, then future relief policy should be altered to give at least intermittent employment, provided that it could be shown that work relief, such as WPA, prevents the pauper attitude. The problem is very complex, but a study of the so-called unemployables and others who have been on relief rolls for a number of years, supplemented by the psychoanalytic study of a considerable number of individuals, might enable us better to understand what constitutes laziness and pauperization.

2. RESEARCH PROBLEMS

In the outline which follows an effort has been made to suggest specific questions regarding subjective responses to the relief experience:

1. What sort of relief workers were assigned to the intake desk?
   (1) Were they professional social workers?
       a. What schools of social work had they attended?
       b. How much social work experience had they had?
       c. In what agencies had they received their experience?
   (2) What is known of their personality characteristics?
       a. Were they sympathetic with the client making application?
       b. Were they equipped with caustic tongues?

    c. Do the records of their interviews indicate that they suspected every applicant to be a malingerer?

    d. Were they patient enough to get a fairly clear picture of the problems of the client before assigning him to a case worker?

(3) What was the age of the intake worker?

(4) What was the marital status of the intake worker? Sex?

(5) In cases showing marked neurotic symptoms, is the experience with the intake worker a factor?

2. What psychological processes during the relief experience affected the degree of cohesion within the family group?

(1) Was fear an important factor?

    a. Fear of displeasing the relief worker?

    b. Fear of losing a work relief job?

    c. Fear on the part of the husband that he would lose status in his own family?

    d. Fear on the part of children that they would lose caste with their former friends who were not on relief?

(2) How important in these processes was the fact of the rapidly changing relief policies?

    a. Was the feeling of insecurity increased?

    b. When changes in relief policy came, did the wife or the children blame the husband for the troubles of the family?

    c. Were the neurotic symptoms of the husband intensified when relief policies changed to make relief less adequate or more uncertain?

(3) What effect did acceptance of dependent status by the wage earner have upon family relations?

    a. Did the wife or children protest this emotional attitude?

    b. Did members of the family adopt the dependent attitude of the wage earner?

    c. What did the case worker do about it?

  (4) What symptoms of hostility were noticed?

    a. In connection with fear responses?

    b. In connection with incomplete acceptance of a dependent status?

    c. Are there cases involving hostility in which the case worker did constructive work?

3. Did the policies of relief administration make it easy for the neurotically inclined to accept a dependent status and find it satisfying?

  (1) How was this fact related to the contacts when the application for relief was first made?

  (2) With what experiences in the development of the individual's personality is this desire for dependency associated?

  (3) When a job in private employment was offered to such a person, did he show symptoms of physical illness?

  (4) From the study of such persons does it appear that the meager case work treatment which was possible, tended to encourage a dependent attitude in the client?

  (5) Could individuals who unconsciously desired a status of dependency have been discovered early and referred for psychiatric treatment?

3. A SUGGESTION REGARDING METHOD

The procedure for this project cannot be illustrated as well as that of some of the other projects. Some of the material in case records can be used to advantage, but for the most part the understanding of the problem will depend upon a large number of cases studied over a period of time by psychiatrists. The

psychoanalytic approach seems to be promising, but it is doubtless not the only possible one. The Institute for Psychoanalysis
in Chicago has carried a number of relief cases which revealed
problems such as those indicated above. One of the cases at
the Institute was that of a young girl who had a work relief job
and was the sole support of her family. During the time she
was working she seemed to have been constantly afraid that the
foreman would dislike her work and would discharge her or
that the project would close and leave her without income. She
developed great tension at times and became embittered because of the hard struggle she was having. She did not accept
dependency but on the contrary developed symptoms characteristic of anxiety neurosis. When these became serious, she came
to the Institute.

A different type of case is indicated by twenty men who were
observed by a member of the Institute staff at a gastro-intestinal
clinic. All of them were on relief, and all of them had stomach
ulcers. Almost all of these men had been well-to-do; some of
them had earned salaries above $10,000 per year. Some of these
men, it was believed, "would never stage a come-back because
their original defenses against dependence . . . had been shat-
tered." They had given in to their tendencies to be dependent.

Such research agencies as the Institute for Psychoanalysis and
perhaps others could make an important contribution toward
the understanding of the social effects of relief policies by undertaking in cooperation with relief agencies the study of a group
of cases exhibiting the symptoms indicated in the description of
this project. The genuine pauper is an individual who has accepted his poverty and has no desire to become economically
and socially independent. He is a neurotic. Have relief policies
tended to increase the number of neurotic persons in the relief
population? That is the problem for research.

Chapter VI

Social Effects of Relief Policies upon Problems of Housing

IN GENERAL, especially prior to the federal period, the attitude of relief agencies regarding rents and the physical condition of houses has been indefinite.

1. POLICY AND PROBLEMS

Only when necessity required it in particular cases was the problem faced. Although less true among good private family relief agencies, they also were chary of it. There are several reasons given for this uncertainty. First, old local public agencies were afraid that landlords, especially large real estate agencies, would exploit the public treasury through pressure; consequently, the agencies prevented this alleged danger from being realized by disregarding problems of rents and housing. Second, it was assumed that the client in most instances had a little income which could be used to pay rent, and this was supposed to stimulate his efforts toward self-maintenance and thereby relieve the agency of some of the relief load as soon as possible. Third, houses were in existence already and would be better cared for with people in them; therefore, the landlord would be compensated in some measure by having caretakers on the place. It appears that prior to the federal period both public and private relief agencies regarded the payment of rent as a less serious obligation than the payment of grocery and clothing bills.

A different problem arose when a family which asked for relief owned the home or had an equity in it. In the pre-federal period a family which owned the home had usually borrowed on it before they sought relief, which necessitated some plan of interest; the mortgagor would generally agree to postponements of payments on the principal. This condition was similar to the situation in which a family found itself, when the home was not fully paid for. In this case interest payments had to be made, though payments on principal could usually be deferred. Then in either situation taxes fell due and eventually had to be paid to save the property. In 1933 the Home Owners Loan Corporation and the agencies of the Agricultural Adjustment Administration came into existence and helped the home owner protect his savings in a considerable proportion of the cases; these federal agencies were, in an important sense, adjuncts to the relief administration.

Landlords who had relief clients paying little or no rent in their houses also found the federal lending agencies important sources of relief for themselves, because they could borrow money for repairs. This relief resource protected property values in some degree.

The housing problem has another important aspect, namely, the quality of houses in which relief clients lived. In the pre-federal period many relief families were living in houses or shacks which had been condemned by boards of health; this fact had some bearing on the rising interest in slum clearance. The experience growing out of relief activities probably accelerated the appropriation of funds for slum clearance projects in many cities; it was certainly a factor in Cincinnati, Cleveland, and Indianapolis. The normally self-maintaining family which went on relief and which had lived in a rented house moved to a less desirable house, except in cases where the landlord reduced the rent or postponed its payment. After the federal period began, a rental allowance was frequently made in the budget, and this enabled more families to continue living in their present homes. At this time also it became possible to include an item in the budget equivalent to rent which the family, if buying a home, might use for interest and tax payments. Among the Negroes in the South the allowance for rent in the budget under federal administration made it possible to live in better houses than formerly, if houses could be found; this may have occurred to a more limited extent among other population groups in cities.

Families were often forced to move out of the houses in which they were living. Sometimes this was due to the usual eviction order, but in the slum clearance projects they had to move because the houses were being demolished to make way for a federal housing project. Landlords were sometimes reluctant to evict a family for several reasons; they sympathized with the plight of the distressed family, they felt that their property would be better protected with some one living in the houses even though no rent was paid, and their inclination to evict a tenant was restrained somewhat by the fear of adverse public reaction. Demolition of houses in slum areas was sometimes delayed because of the difficulty of finding places for tenants to live, many of whom were receiving relief. It would be interesting to know what kind of accommodations were found for clients who were evicted by landlords, or who had to move because of slum clearance projects. When the new housing projects are completed, it would also be interesting to know how the economic and social status of the new tenants compares with that of the tenants of the demolished houses. The Works Progress Administration made a pre-demolition survey of residents in a slum clearance area in Minneapolis, and the Colored Young Men's Christian Association of Indianapolis made a similar survey in the Negro housing area in that city.

2. RESEARCH PROBLEMS

The study of the housing problem in relation to relief policies is very complex, but the following outline suggests an approach to it:

1. In the pre-federal period how were rents handled by relief agencies?
   (1) To what extent did private relief agencies pay rents?
   (2) How did private relief agencies handle situations in which the home was owned or the family had an equity in it?
   (3) By what process of reasoning did the private agencies arrive at their rental policies?
   (4) How much rent was paid by public relief agencies?
   (5) How did the public relief agencies handle the case, when the home was owned or the family had an equity in it?
   (6) What were the reasons back of the rental policies of public agencies?
2. In the federal period how were rents handled by relief agencies?
   (1) Was the federal policy of paying rents carried out by state and local agencies?
   (2) In what proportion of cases was it possible for families to continue living in the same houses they had at the time of application for relief?
   (3) What percentage of the total budget was allowed for rent?
   (4) Under what circumstances, if any, was payment of rent refused?
   (5) What was the experience of real estate agencies during this period, and how did it vary from the pre-federal period?
   (6) How important was the allowance of a rental equivalent in the budget which the relief family might use for payment of interest on the mortgage or payment of taxes?
3. During the federal period what were the relations between the local relief agencies and the federal lending agencies?

    (1) Did the relief agencies advise clients on means of obtaining loans to save their property?

    (2) If federal loans were obtained, did the relief agency include a rental-equivalent item in the budget to aid in making the monthly payments of interest, principal and taxes?

4. What difference existed between the quality of houses of relief clients and the quality of houses the same people lived in before going on relief?

    (1) In the pre-federal period did relief agencies allow families to live in houses condemned by the health authorities?

    (2) Was there any difference in this practice during the federal period?

    (3) After going on relief did clients move from one house to another on their own initiative or at the suggestion of the relief agency? If the former, why did they move? How much moving was there?

5. Did overcrowding occur in relief families?

    (1) What was the number of persons per room?

    (2) Was there a tendency toward doubling up of relief families? Any geographical or racial differences?

    (3) Were newlyweds among clients encouraged to live by themselves or to live with the parents of one of them?

6. How did work relief affect the housing of clients?

    (1) After having received direct relief for a time, if a family went on work relief, did it move to a better house or neighborhood?

    (2) Did work relief enable some families to keep the homes which they were buying?

    (3) Did some families begin buying homes out of work-relief incomes?

    (4) If families owed back rent for the houses in which

they were living, did they attempt to pay it, when they got work relief, or did they evade it by moving?

7. Is there any evidence that the traditional policy of relief agencies to refuse to pay rent developed a similar attitude toward this obligation in the client?

(1) Did the client, following the relief agency, come to regard the landlord as a legitimate object for exploitation?

(2) What bearing have the eviction laws upon the possible development of this attitude?

8. What happened to families which were forcibly moved out of their houses?

(1) Those evicted by landlords:

a. What influenced the landlord to evict one client, and not evict another, although both were in arrears with their rent?

b. Where did the evicted clients stay the night after eviction?

c. What kind of houses were found by or for evicted clients?

d. Did the landlords find that it was better to have non-rent-paying clients in their houses than to have the houses vacant?

e. What proportion of evicted clients moved into houses with other families?

f. After an eviction did the relief agency regularly pay rent in order to get the client settled?

g. How did the quality of the new homes compare with that of those from which the clients were evicted?

h. What was the attitude of the courts and sheriffs toward giving or executing an eviction order?

i. Can the public attitude toward evictions be determined?

(2) Those moved to make way for a slum clearance project:
   a. What assistance in finding new homes was given the clients by relief agencies?
   b. In what proportion of the cases did they double up with other families?
   c. Was the family sometimes broken up by agreement?
   d. How did the quality of their houses before and after removal compare?
   e. In completed housing projects did some of the old residents of the area, including clients, move into the new houses?

3. NOTE ON METHOD

A brief perusal of the foregoing questions will suggest that the methods of approach and the sources of data are various. The possible ramifications of this project can be illustrated by reference to the fourth question: "What differences existed between the quality of houses of relief clients and the quality of houses the same people lived in before going on relief?" Extensive studies of housing have been done in a number of cities in connection with slum clearance projects, one of the most comprehensive of which was done under the auspices of the Cleveland Health Council under the direction of Howard Whipple Green. Several series of social and economic data were distributed by census tracts, rates per population were computed, spot maps were made, and averages and correlation coefficients computed. High relief rates are associated with high rates for other social problems and are concentrated in areas of low grade houses. The data used by the Health Council were obtained from such sources as their own health records, the city department of health, the relief agencies, the courts, the utility companies, and real estate offices. Similar statistical studies, very often done on work relief projects, have been made in other cities. The Cleveland study does not answer specifically the fourth question above, but some of the same kind of data used in that study will be required to answer this question. In addition, however, more information will have to be obtained from case records in order to trace the housing experience of clients; these data are in the case records, because they were important facts in making family budgets and in dealing with landlords and had to be recorded.

Chapter VII

Social Effects of Relief Policies upon Institution Populations[1]

INSTITUTIONAL relief policies have been chiefly the concern of local and state governments. Certain kinds of relief to war veterans are exceptions, but the amount of this kind of relief is relatively small. The policies of the Federal Emergency Relief Administration might have an indirect bearing upon the movement of population in institutions because of limitations upon the use of federal funds, but there has been no direct connection; on the contrary federal relief policies, as stated in the Social Security Act, would have the effect of reducing the number of children, aged persons and blind persons in institutions. State and county policies have undoubtedly had a variety of direct effects on institutional populations. In the early days of the depression the almshouse provided a sort of workhouse test for applicants for relief; this was especially true in the case of homeless men. In this same period shelters for homeless and transient men were often filled to capacity; later the federal government allowed funds for this type of relief. If the shelters and the camps established under the federal transient program are regarded as institutions, then federal policy for a short time did include institutional relief for a class of clients.

1. POLICIES AND PROBLEMS

But besides almshouses, poor asylums, poor farms and shelters, relief policies may have affected other types of institutions.

---

[1] In connection with this chapter the reader is referred to monographs in this series on social work, crime, and social aspects of health.

In most states the hospitals for the insane are always crowded, but there is some opinion that the applications for admission to these institutions increased during the depression: families trying to live on a small relief allowance attempted to get their psychotics and neurotics admitted to the hospitals; and milder psychoneurotics sometimes attempted to gain admission on their own initiative for treatment, though these would be small in number. It is possible that private homes for the aged found their applications increasing; most of them are always full, and their actual average attendance during the depression may not have varied much from predepression years. Little is known whether or not relief policies have affected the population in penal and correctional institutions, but because of the fact that for a number of years parole boards have been reluctant to parole a man or young person without a job in sight the average daily attendance may have increased. This also may have tended to lengthen the average time in the institutions.

Aside from the mere number of persons who were admitted to public welfare institutions, the type of person admitted is of considerable interest. Before the WPA made the classification, "employable" and "unemployable," local relief administrators had used the concept more loosely. Has there been a tendency throughout the depression for relief agencies to send many of their unemployables to institutions? Not only the type of person admitted but also the number of times he was admitted and discharged is important. Instead of encouraging the ordinary dependency, relief policies might have had the effect in an appreciable number of cases of stimulating individuals to criminal and delinquent behavior, and recidivism may have become more frequent. These are possible direct or indirect effects of relief policies, which are not often thought about but which are worth studying sufficiently to answer the query.

If able-bodied, employable persons have been sent to institutions instead of giving them outdoor relief, two other questions are raised. In some localities the cost of keeping an individual in an institution is considerably greater than giving him outdoor relief. (It will not be difficult to determine the relative costs of the two forms of relief.) Furthermore, if an employable person is kept in an institution, he is cut off from the labor market and has less opportunity to secure employment in private industry. The extent to which this occurred is important in formulating future relief policies which involve both indoor and outdoor relief. In some states the inmates of almshouses are classified according to the reasons for admission, and statistics of the almshouse population in the early years of the depression show the percentage of inmates who were admitted for no other reason than unemployment; a reverse trend may have begun with the opening of the federal period. Since this group of people were merely given food and shelter, it would be desirable to compare the adequacy of the service received in the almshouse with what they would normally have received from outdoor relief. The almshouse has the reputation of giving the lowest grade of relief service, and it is possible that people entered them in good health and left them with reduced capacity for work.

2. RESEARCH PROBLEMS

Let us state the direction which research might take more definitely:

1. What effects did relief policies have upon the almshouse population?
    (1) Was there an increase in the almshouse population after 1929?
        a. In the percentage of able-bodied persons admitted?
        b. Because of a decrease in the rate of turnover?
        c. How did the increase compare with the rate of increase in the general relief load?
        d. Were some almshouses closed as unnecessary or too expensive?
    (2) Did the composition of the almshouse population change?

    a. How did the age distribution compare with the age distribution before the depression?

    b. What was the sex distribution?

    c. How did the percentages of the classes by reasons for admission compare with similar percentages before the depression?

    d. Was there cooperation between outdoor and indoor relief authorities in determining policies?

(3) How did residence in the almshouse affect the health of inmates?

    a. What was the condition of their health at the time of admission?

    b. Is the state of their health at the time of discharge known?

    c. What communicable diseases did they contract while in the almshouse?

    d. Can the health of almshouse inmates be compared with similar groups on outdoor relief?

(4) How did costs of almshouse relief compare with outdoor relief costs?

    a. Food?   d. Health?

    b. Shelter?   e. Miscellaneous relief?

    c. Clothing?   f. Administration?

(5) How did residence in the almshouse affect the opportunities of the inmate to get private employment?

    a. Were the able-bodied registered with the public employment service?

    b. How did the able-bodied inmates learn of jobs?

    c. Did residence in an almshouse prejudice a prospective employer against the inmate?

2. Did relief policies have any important effects upon institutional populations other than the almshouse?

(1) What was the experience of free general hospitals?

    a. Did the number of inpatients increase?

    b. How did the hospital days per patient compare

with hospital days per patient before the depression?

c. To what extent did the policies of the relief agencies tend to increase hospitalization in free hospitals?

d. Was special attention given to maternity cases?

(2) Did hospitals for the care of mental cases feel the effects of relief policies?

a. Increased number of admissions?

b. Increased number of applications for admission of seniles and other mild forms of mental disorder?

c. Increased rate of turnover of patients as a response to pressure of relief agencies to get clients admitted?

d. Do hospital superintendents feel that relief policies may have aggravated the disturbance of persons who finally were admitted?

e. Because of the widespread relief organization, was it possible for hospitals to furlough patients sooner and to depend upon the relief agencies to give them some supervision?

(3) Did relief policies affect commitments to and discharges from penal and correctional institutions?

a. By providing inadequate relief budgets which led to stealing?

b. By forcing the doubling up of families, which increased irritations and, possibly, crimes against the person?

c. By delaying parole because family was on relief and chance of rehabilitation thereby reduced?

d. Did they increase the ratio of misdemeanors to felonies and, hence, lead to relatively greater overcrowding of jails and other correctional institutions?

(4) How did relief policies affect the population of institutions for dependent and neglected children?

    a. Were more children accepted for adoption?

    b. Did more parents seek to have their children admitted?

    c. Has the population decreased since Title IV of the Social Security Act became effective?

    d. Did the admission rate decline when more adequate relief became available through federal grants?

3. NOTE ON METHOD

There are many official reports showing the tabulations of data which have a bearing upon the problems suggested above. These reports do not ordinarily attempt to show a connection between institutional cases and relief policies. A good example of this kind of statistical report is the *Annual Statistical Review of Patients with Mental Disease in the State Hospitals and Licensed Institutions, Year Ended June 30, 1935,* for New York State. In 1930 and 1931 the annual increase of patients in all institutions fell off, but in 1932 the corresponding figure was almost fifty per cent higher than in 1931, and it was still higher in 1933 and 1934. When the Psychiatric Institute and Hospital was opened in 1931, there was a sharp increase in the percentage of voluntary patients in the state; whether or not this increased number of voluntary admissions in New York City had anything to do with relief policies cannot be determined from the published data. From 1928 onward the percentage of patients on furlough remained fairly constant. After 1931 there was a relatively large increase in first admissions, and this resulted mainly from increased first admissions with general paresis, psychoses with cerebral arteriosclerosis, involutional psychoses and the psychoneuroses. It is possible that some of these have a definite relation to the stress and strain of the relief experience, but it would be necessary to study the history of the specific cases in order to determine it. All such cases would have to be checked against the relief rolls, and an examination of the case records would be required to discover the action of the agency.

Chapter VIII

Social Effects of Relief Policies upon Minority Groups[1]

THERE is considerable opinion to the effect that certain minority groups have been discriminated against by relief agencies. Negroes, Chinese, Japanese, Filipinos, Mexicans, foreign-born citizens and aliens generally are regarded in many communities as an inferior class in the population which is not entitled to the ordinary rights of the general population. Furthermore, unattached women and certain small, political groups were treated as minority groups against whom discrimination was sanctioned. Relief status in some localities led to denial of certain civil rights.

1. POLICIES

The degree of prejudice against these groups varies in different localities, but in some states it is intense and general. Prejudice against the Negro in the South is institutionalized, and the same observation can be made regarding Chinese, Japanese and Filipinos in certain western cities. Prejudice against foreign-born citizens and aliens is less definitely localized. It is to be expected that, when relief was required by a family of one of these minority groups, some consideration would be given to the prevailing attitude in the community. This is more likely to have been widespread in the pre-federal period than after the Federal Emergency Relief Administration came into exist-

---

[1] For proposed research on the effects of the depression in general on minority groups see Young, Donald. *Research Memorandum on Minority Peoples in the Depression.* (monograph in this series)

ence. Private relief agencies in the early part of the depression may have pursued policies different from those of local public agencies with respect to minority groups. This cannot be assumed, however, because the standards of relief in private agencies were higher than they were in public agencies, and the ratio of the amount of relief in general to the amount of relief for minority groups may not have differed much from the corresponding ratio in the public agencies.

The problem of assuring fair treatment of minority groups was recognized very early in the rules and regulations of the Federal Emergency Relief Administration. On July 11, 1933, (Rules and Regulations No. 3) the administrator's instructions to the states included the following references to administration of relief: "Relief shall be given as provided in this Act to all needy unemployed persons and/or their dependents. Those whose employment or available resources are inadequate to provide the necessities of life for themselves and/or their dependents are included," and again in the same order, "There shall be no discrimination because of race, religion, color, non-citizenship, political affiliation, or because of membership in any special or selected group." These orders are general and inclusive. If discrimination existed after a state began to receive federal aid, it was a result of the policy and practice of the state or local relief agency; no subsequent statement of policy by the federal administration can be interpreted as permitting discrimination.

In the study of this problem a special consideration immediately arises. In general it may be said that Negroes, Mexicans, Chinese, Filipinos and to a less extent Japanese have a lower standard of living than the general population in the communities where they live. To an important extent this is also true for aliens and other foreign-born persons, but it is less true of those persons born in the north of Europe. The recognition of the usual standard of living of these minority groups has influenced the practice of local relief agencies, and in many localities the officials are frank to state that the relief allowance was determined with a view to maintaining a fraction of the usual standard of living. Consequently, minority group cases involving five persons, for example, get somewhat less than a family of five from the majority group of the population. In the early stages of federal relief, cases from minority groups were given the same direct relief allowance or work relief wages as others, but it was observed that this provided a standard of living higher than some of these families had ever had from their own earnings; this observation led to a reduction in the amount of relief for these families.

2. PROBLEMS

The foregoing consideration complicates the conception of discrimination. A working definition, more general than that which is merely based upon difference in quantity of relief, seems to be necessary, before the research worker can begin the study of the problem outlined here. Probably all states had theoretical food budgets made up by home economists for families of varying size; the other items in the theoretical budget were less scientifically constructed. But there were general family budgets, and the relief allowance for the majority group in the population was either the amount of the theoretical budget or some fraction of it. In the pre-federal period these budgets were taken less seriously in most states, chiefly because the traditional relief officials knew little about budgets, but in the federal period they became standardized. However, the fraction of the theoretical budget which was allowed minority groups was likely to be smaller than it was in the case of the families of the majority groups. Aliens and foreign-born citizens from Europe in most localities probably found themselves receiving allowances similar to those of the majority group, but there is ground for suspecting that in some localities they received consideration for work relief opportunities after the majority group had been placed. Consequently, there are two sides to the idea of discrimination: one is the fact of having a smaller allowance for cases from the minority group; and the other is the fact of taking into account the usual standard of living of the minority group in determining the allowance, whereas this was done only in isolated cases in the majority group.

It is an important problem, therefore, of the social effects of relief policy to discover the extent to which discrimination against minority groups existed during the depression. That it existed is admitted by local relief officials in many states. All the forms of discrimination are probably not well known, and in the course of studying the amount of discrimination care should be taken to identify less common modes of discrimination. Since prejudices against different racial and nationality groups vary in different localities, it will be necessary, in any locality where a study of discrimination is undertaken, to determine what groups are disliked and, hence, constitute minority groups as defined here. The case records will usually indicate the race or nationality of the family, and the attached budget and financial record will show what allowance and other service the case received. Files of the complaint division of the relief office may have valuable information on discrimination.

Because relief has been for several years the major governmental activity in all states, it was the concern of all citizens. To what extent, then, did representatives of minority groups participate with other citizens in the determination of local relief policies and in the administration of relief? Private relief agencies have for many years attempted to have the membership of their boards representative of all important groups in the community, and the staffs of the larger private agencies have in some degree reflected the racial and nationality composition of the local population. The old public relief agencies paid less attention to this matter. Since so many former employees of private agencies were drafted into the depression relief service of public agencies, it would be interesting to know to what extent they introduced the practice of having wide representation of the community on their advisory committees and on their staffs. In some of the southern states, at least, it became necessary to employ some Negro case workers, but it is not clear that the Negro community had much influence in the determination of local policies. The same question can be raised about the Mexicans in the Southwest and in California, about the Chinese on the Pacific Coast and in large eastern cities, and about other foreign-born groups. Personnel records, minutes of meetings and lists of the membership of advisory committees exist in abundance for the study of this question.

A special kind of discrimination to which the alien was exposed was the threat, or the fact, of deportation. During 1930, 1931 and 1932 the United States Department of Labor made a vigorous effort to find and to deport aliens—this aggressive policy was abandoned after March 4, 1933. Some of these aliens had married citizens and had children born in this country, but there are believed to be many cases on record of such aliens being deported and forced to abandon their families here without means of support or without the effective interest of both parents. This seems to have been one way of removing employed aliens from jobs so that unemployed citizens could have them and of removing a few dependent aliens from the relief rolls. After the Federal Emergency Relief Act was passed, aliens were entitled to get relief. It would be an interesting study to find out how many persons deported were taken from relief rolls both before and after this Act went into effect.

Because of the fear of deportation, many aliens seem to have taken out naturalization papers. So long as it was not necessary for them to apply for relief, they were comparatively safe, but one of the questions asked by relief agencies, both before and during the depression, relates to place of birth and citizenship. In many places classes under the auspices of the relief administration were conducted for aliens and other foreign-born persons. A good deal of this work was undertaken specifically for the purpose of preparing aliens to take the citizenship examinations. It would be easy to determine from immigration statistics what the trend of naturalization was during the depression, but to show the effects of this trend on local relief policies toward aliens, it would be necessary to trace the names of those naturalized through the relief rolls. This kind of study might show that an application for relief followed soon after the first citizenship papers were taken out and, hence, would suggest action taken to prepare the individual for eligibility for relief, in the event that he had to ask for it.

It is widely believed that unattached women and members of certain minor political groups were treated as minority groups and that considerable discrimination against them existed. Because of the ancient belief that the woman's place was in the home, it is possible that discrimination against unattached women was unintentional and a result of the blind assumption that every woman had a home to which she could go and, hence, be a member of a family. Such women certainly did not occupy a large place in the program for transients and homeless persons. Furthermore, in some localities it is believed that clients suffered a de facto loss of some of their usual civil rights. Expressions of contempt for radical groups and of the conviction that they were not entitled to receive relief were not uncommon; whether or not the relief agencies followed the lead of these expressed attitudes is something to be determined.

3. RESEARCH PROBLEMS

The following outline will suggest more specifically an approach to the study of minority groups in relation to relief policies:

1. What kinds of discrimination against minority groups existed in relief agencies?

(1) Did they receive smaller food allowances?

(2) Did they receive rental allowances in proportion to their numbers?

(3) Were they certified for work relief in proportion to their numbers?

(4) Were milk and special diets provided?

(5) Were the young men certified for the CCC?

(6) Were alien applications reported to the deportation authorities?

(7) Were clothes for school children in such families given out less freely than to children in other families?

2. What was the extent of discrimination in such categories as those indicated under No. 1?

3. Did minority groups have a voice in proportion to their numbers in the determination of relief administration?

(1) Did their representatives serve on advisory committees?

(2) Did the agencies select a proportionate number of case workers from these groups?

(3) Were representatives of minority groups in supervisory positions in the relief agencies?

4. What effects did relief policies have upon deportation and naturalization of aliens?

(1) What has been the trend of naturalization during the depression?

(2) How many recently naturalized persons were on the relief rolls?

(3) Is there evidence in case records that the relief agencies resented the application of a recently naturalized alien?

(4) Did relief agencies report alien applicants to the U. S. Department of Labor for deportation?

(5) Has the U. S. Department of Labor sent inspectors

to examine relief rolls in the search for aliens in
order to deport them?

5. To what extent were certain nonracial groups treated as
minority groups against whom discrimination was sanctioned?

(1) Unattached women?

(2) Political groups, such as communists?

(3) Clients in so far as civil rights were concerned?

6. How many of the persons deported were on relief rolls at
the time they were apprehended? Was there any charge
other than dependency placed against them?

4. NOTE ON METHOD

That proof of discrimination against a minority group may
be difficult is illustrated by a study made by the Federal Emergency Relief Administration, entitled *The Rural Negro on Relief, February, 1935* (Serial No. H-3). Forty-four sample counties were taken in the eastern and western cotton areas, and in
these counties there were 17,153 white and 8,266 Negro relief
households. It was found that Negro relief cases were under-
represented on work relief projects and that they got less direct
relief per household than the white families. In the open country
Negroes made up 33 per cent of the total case load but only 19
per cent of the work relief cases; in villages they made up 38
per cent of the case load but only 31 per cent of the work relief
cases; in the small towns they made up 40 per cent of the total
case load but only 37 per cent of the work relief cases. On direct
relief for all cases the average amount of relief in the eastern
area for white families was $13.00 and for Negro families was
$10.00 and in the western area the corresponding figures were
$11.00 and $9.00. Is there any explanation of differences? The
relatively small number of Negro families represented on work
relief is partly accounted for by the fact that the size of each

Negro household was 3.78, whereas the size of each white household was 4.33, and further by the fact that among the cases eligible for employment 11.7 per cent of the whites had no male worker, whereas 21.0 per cent of such Negro cases had no male worker. When an analysis of families on direct relief was made by size of family it was found that the white families received about $1.00 per person more per month than did Negro families per person in the household—the difference was a little less in some classifications. On the basis of these and other facts the study concludes: "The data of the present study has shown that a surprisingly large amount of the difference in representation of whites and Negroes in the relief population may be accounted for on the basis of such factors as differences in employability composition, current employment opportunities, size of relief case, and differences in scales of living." No claims are made by this study to finality. It is one of many sample studies which the FERA has conducted, using the data provided by the local relief staffs. Such a term as, "employability," can, of course, be interpreted with reference to a Negro to fit the local prejudices, and in so far as some Negroes were adjudged unemployable objective evidence for the decision is required. The phrase, "differences in scales of living," also reflects the local decision to base Negro relief upon what was conceived to be their proper standard of living. Such terms as these, when found in a relief record, require critical appraisal. The research worker will have to dig into much background material to determine their meaning and, hence, to measure the effects of relief policies on the Negro.

Chapter IX

Social Effects of Relief Policies upon Community Organization

THE phrase, "community organization," is currently used to refer to the organization of agencies and other resources in any political unit or subdivision or any other area for the attainment of community objectives. In practice, therefore, the term may refer to a township, a municipality, a county, a state or the nation, and in this proposed study it will involve several of them at the same time. The factors included in community organization are finance, agencies, personnel, laws and geographical areas. The adoption or alteration of relief policies produces a variety of combinations of these factors.

1. POLICIES

In the early years of the depression relief policies were concerned almost exclusively with the organization of local community units. Private social agencies, especially those in cities, expanded through the use of their boards of directors, and by the creation of special committees of citizens. Their aim was to raise a maximum amount of money by voluntary subscription in order to provide reasonably adequate relief to as large a number of cases as possible. During the same period, township, municipal and county governments enlarged their budgets in order to provide relief according to their customary standards. By 1931 and 1932 states were setting up relief administrations to assist local governmental units in financing and administering relief. Up to 1932 private relief agencies sought larger and larger contributions from their supporters, and the local public agencies sold bonds and levied taxes to meet the demands made upon them. Grants-in-aid from state governments began to increase. In 1932 the federal government made loans through the Reconstruction Finance Corporation. The RFC relief functions continued in force until the passage of the Federal Emergency Relief Act in May, 1933. On May 23, 1933, the administrator notified the states that thereafter the federal government would make to any state a grant-in-aid equal to one-third of the relief expenditures in the state during the first quarter of that year. The proportion of the cost of relief paid by the federal government increased until it was more than three-fourths of the total expenditure in some states; the fixed ratio soon passed into disuse. Methods of financing the nonfederal portion of relief costs varied. The relations between the different levels of relief administration shifted several times and varied at the same time in different localities. As work relief became more important, two relief administrations existed side by side, one concerned with direct relief and the other with work relief; when the WPA was created, this dichotomy became definite and legal, with the states and local units providing direct relief and the federal government assuming responsibility for the work relief program. Relief status was unsettled when special agencies were created for drought relief and rural resettlement which partly or completely replaced existing agencies. After the federal government stepped into the relief situation policies changed frequently. With each major change of policy came a shake-up in community organization. Functions, powers and financial obligations had to be redefined and adjustments made to carry out the functions, exercise the powers and raise the funds.

Attention should be directed to federal grants as "equalization funds." They did function as such, because the percentage of relief funds coming from federal sources differed widely among the states. Incidentally, the Association of Community

Chests and Councils has undertaken to study this problem for private social agencies and to lay out a plan by which a large corporation might make a single contribution and have it pro-rated to community chests of cities in which its business is conducted. Because no clear principle has been stated for government equalization funds and because the existence of such a need has been implicit in the federal program, it is important that the subject be studied with a view to the determination of a reasonable basis upon which to organize and administer equalization funds. This problem arises in federal-state relations and in state-county relations.

A comprehensive study of the problems of community organization arising out of the experience with relief, needs to be made. Because of the necessity of giving immediate relief to millions of families, time was not available for the proper consideration of these problems during the worst part of the depression, but the data for their study are abundant and can now be analyzed at leisure. An evaluation of relief policies as they affected community organization is important for the development of permanent plans for general relief and for any future expansion of relief administration in order to cope with an emergency.

2. PROBLEMS

Pressure groups of varying size and importance arose in many parts of the country and often exercised far-reaching influence. In the early years of the depression these pressure groups consisted of clients trying to get more adequate relief or to prevent eviction, of radical groups making the most of local social unrest, of citizens representing private social agencies which were trying to get governmental agencies to assume a larger proportion of the relief burden and of officials trying to get assistance from higher units of government. There was, of course, some counter pressure to hold relief expenditures to a minimum. By the time the new federal administration came into power in 1933, the pressure for more money had become so nearly unanimous that it was politically desirable for congressmen and senators to favor large appropriations for relief; candidates were elected often on a platform which predicated adequate relief appropriations by Congress. Although we know in general the lines of pressure, we do not know the relative importance of pressure groups or the kinds of pressure brought to bear upon governments. The Townsend movement to secure old-age pensions of $200.00 per month per person had its roots in the experience with relief, and there is some evidence in the Townsend literature to suggest that its original drive had its origin in dissatisfaction with relief to old people. It would be desirable to know to what extent efforts to establish other forms of categorical relief, such as aid to the blind and to dependent children, derive from the mass experience with general relief. The discussion of unemployment insurance increased immensely after the depression became serious; the Wisconsin law, the first of its kind in this country, was passed in 1932 after more than ten years of organized effort to place it on the statute books. Then came the Federal Social Security Act which established a vast system of social insurance and categorical relief. Legislation for old-age pensions, pensions for the blind and mothers' pensions had gained some headway in the states before 1929, but old-age insurance and unemployment insurance were mainly subjects for academic discussion. The fact that President Roosevelt believed strongly in this type of legislation contributed to the rapid growth of popular opinion favorable to it, but the tremendous Democratic majority in the 1936 election suggests that, in spite of the last minute attack on the Social Security Act by the Republicans, there is general support of comprehensive social legislation. Not all pressure exerted was for greater relief expenditures. As the volume of relief aid increased powerful and influential groups made known their interest in lower relief costs and criticized the federal program. Pressure from this direction reached its climax in the presidential campaign in which the character and extent of federal aid was probably a major issue.

Data for an objective study of pressure groups will be difficult to get, because there are so many imponderables involved, but the Townsend literature is available, newspaper reports and editorials can be studied, local popular votes for candidates can be obtained, and the votes on bills for social legislation in Congress and the state legislatures are obtainable. Such information as this would constitute some check on an evalution of the less tangible evidence which has a bearing upon public opinion.

Changes in the relative importance of taxing units mark another important alteration in community organization. Back of relief polices, of course, stands the depression itself, but the changes in the taxing units came because of the policy of providing subsistence for all individuals and families without income. Ordinary governmental budgets declined in response to the restriction of national income and the general decrease in property values. These could be cut at various points without endangering the morale and the health of the community, but the provision of relief was the sine qua non of morale and health, and it necessitated total public budgets higher than had obtained during prosperous times. The dilemma of reduced ability to pay taxes and the necessity of more public money for relief of the unemployed led both to borrowing and to increased taxes. Local taxing units on whom responsibility for relief had traditionally fallen declared that they were unable to finance relief; states, due to a mixture of political and economic reasons, protested that they could not raise enough money to supplement local requirements and that, therefore, the only way out was for the federal government to assume the major responsibility for the cost of relief.

It was apparent in 1932 that the majority of the population accepted the proposition that relief was a federal responsibility.

This shift in public opinion regarding the organization of con-centric communities for taxation purposes can, fortunately for the researcher, be checked against public financial records. Trends in the proportion of relief paid for by municipalities, townships, towns, counties, states and the federal government can be stated statistically. This problem gains its significance not only from the fact that the relative importance of taxing units for relief purposes has changed but also from the fact that it has a definite bearing upon the centralization of government, because power follows control over public financial resources and the right to spend.

Another problem closely allied with the changing importance of the taxing unit is the change in the kinds of taxes used to finance the cost of relief. The relative importance of former taxes has changed, and new kinds of taxes have been invented or extended during the depression. Taxes have changed and new taxes have been invented, because the ingenuity of public officials has been strained to discover ways of paying the cost of relief. The general property tax has declined in importance in many states. Taxes on intangibles—e.g., bonds, stock certificates, mortgages, etc.—have been added. Net income and inheritance taxes have found increasing favor among legislators. One state has a gross income tax. Head taxes have been levied for a particular kind of relief. Excise and sales taxes have proliferated throughout the nation, some of them earmarked for relief. Financial relief of the local community has usu-ally implied a substitution of some new state or federal tax for a part of the general property tax. Grants-in-aid by either the federal government or state governments have been fi-nanced out of taxes other than property taxes, and these grants-in-aid are becoming institutionalized in the establishment of machinery to carry on categorical relief and social insurance. This fact is clearly one of the evidences of the growing cen-tralization of government, and it has an important bearing upon public administration in general. Studies of this problem have already been undertaken, but a full understanding of its nature and importance is still in the future.[1]

Legal settlement laws have created some of the most difficult problems of local relief administration. Before the federal period the principal conflict was between the potential client and the local overseer of the poor; individuals and families without legal settlement in the locality in which they sought relief usually had to appeal to the private agencies. But when the federal program got under way, the policy of providing relief for any one who needed it was adopted. Federal money could be used to relieve any person in need irrespective of citizenship, not to say legal settlement. This led to the development of the federal program for transients and homeless persons.

When direct relief was abandoned by the federal government in 1935, the old problems of legal settlement came to the front again. Gradually, however, some compromise was reached in most communities by which persons without legal settlement could obtain at least temporary relief. Efforts were made to determine the place of legal settlement of the client, and, in cases where this could be established, overseers of the poor often sent the clients back to their places of legal settlement, or at least gave them a ticket "in that direction," a practice which left some clients stranded again in places where they had no legal settlement. A few states have never had legal settlement laws, but some others require a residence of several years to establish the right to relief from local public agencies. This confusion has led to proposals in states with long-residential requirements for a liberalization or abolition of laws of legal settlement, but in some of the states without such laws there has been some sentiment in favor of enactment of statutes regard-

---

[1] See Wells, Anita. *Distribution of Relief Funds between the Political Subdivisions of the States.* Washington, D.C.: WPA. Municipal Finance Section. Division of Research, Statistics, and Records. July 1936

ing legal settlement. The whole problem deserves a more thorough study than it has yet had. We need to know how many applicants for relief lacked legal settlement in the localities in which they made application, what were the special problems created, what the temporary solutions were, what the experience of states without legal settlement laws was and what changes have been made in the statutes. There should be no difficulty in securing data for the study of the problem, because most of the information required is a matter of public record.

A much debated question is that of the effects of public relief policies upon private social agencies. Most of the large family welfare societies have adopted a policy of restricting their case loads to a smaller number of families requiring services other than relief. This change in policy permitted a reduction in their customary budgets and in personnel, but it was followed by a larger cost per case because more intensive work was being done. Contributions to community chests reached a peak in the autumn of 1931 and the spring of 1932, that is, in funds raised for the year 1932; after 1932 they declined sharply to the levels of 1928 and 1929. Among community chests there has also been more emphasis upon the so-called "character-building agencies"; in some cities, at least, these agencies have received relatively large allotments from the contributions to community chests. A study of contributions to community chests, of the number and kind of private agencies, of the shifts in budgets by kinds of private agencies and of the relations of the private agencies to the public relief agencies is much needed to clarify the division of labor between private and public social agencies and to define more clearly the proper functions of private social work. Some of the material required for such a study is contained in statistical and case records, but some of it is more intangible. However, there are data adequate for a worthwhile study of the problem.[2]

[2] See Chapin, F. Stuart, and Queen, Stuart A. *Research Memorandum on Social Work in the Depression.*

Much has been said in recent years about the use of leisure time, and it has been the policy of relief administrations at various times during the depression to do something about the long days of unoccupied time of the unemployed.[3] Before the federal period private recreational agencies found their limited facilities overburdened by the increased attendance upon their activities and by the greater demands for means of passing the time or finding diversion from worries. The local relief agencies in the early years of the depression rarely gave attention to leisure-time problems, but in some communities the public school authorities made buildings available for use in the evenings. On August 19, 1933, the emergency education program was announced by the FERA, and it included provision for the payment of unemployed teachers who would conduct classes for adult illiterates. This was extended September 26 to include vocational and general educational classes composed of unemployed persons. A little later instructions went out that the transient service should provide recreational activities for its clients. As work relief became more important, projects for work on parks and playgrounds were approved. State relief administrations appointed state and local advisory committees to plan the leisure-time programs, some of which received the unqualified praise of leaders in the leisure-time field. These developments were more noticeable in urban centers than in rural communities. In the cities, parks and playgrounds were improved and often extended, public buildings were utilized for recreational purposes, the variety of facilities for leisure-time activities increased, participation in adult education was greater, and a multiplication of group activities occurred. There seemed to be a general acceptance on a wider scale of the theory that a constructive use of leisure time is a proper concern of government. The organization of leisure-time activities and the opera-

[3] For a more detailed treatment of this problem see Steiner, Jesse F. *Research Memorandum on Recreation in the Depression.* (monograph in this series)

tion of work relief projects in connection with them received much attention, because they were in a sense mass activities. A study of these should be made to determine their importance in the scheme of community organization. Data for the study of the emergency educational program are easily available in the records of this service and additions to the physical equipment of recreational facilities can be determined from an examination of project records, but the only measurement of participation in activities commonly called recreational is attendance, which is not very reliable. Some evaluation of the whole program, however, could be made.

3. RESEARCH PROBLEMS

Breaking these problems down into more specific questions, they appear as follows:
1. Pressure groups arising out of the relief experience:
    (1) What kinds of pressure led to the establishment of federal relief?
        a. Local disorders which disturbed local officials?
        b. Representations of citizens' committees?
        c. Pressure of local officials upon state officials for financial relief?
        d. Pressure of state administrations upon the federal administration? Mayors? Governors?
        e. Discovery by congressional candidates that promises of relief had vote-getting possibilities?
    (2) Were local pressure groups instrumental in getting relief budgets increased?
        a. Pressure by Unemployed Citizens' Leagues?
        b. Pressure by Unemployed Workers' Alliance?
        c. Pressure by socialist or communist groups?
        d. Pressure from owners of real estate to get a rent item in the budget?
        e. Pressure from temporary aggregations of clients?

(3) Did experience with relief for the aged stimulate the movement for old-age pensions?
  a. The Townsend movement?
  b. Activities of the Eagles Lodge?
  c. Activities of the American Association for Social Security?

(4) Was experience with relief related to the growth of the movement for other forms of categorical relief, such as:
  a. Pensions for the blind?
  b. Aid to dependent children in their own homes?
  c. Special assistance to veterans?

(5) How was the relief experience related to the rapid growth of sentiment for unemployment insurance?
  a. Arguments used in the early years of the depression in Wisconsin for the unemployment insurance bill?
  b. Report of the Ohio Commission?
  c. Activities of the Conference of six states called by Governor Roosevelt?
  d. Published articles and books relating to foreign experience with unemployment insurance?

(6) To what extent were clients organized by local political leaders and officials to support the incumbent party?
  a. On the grounds that the client owed his assistance to that party?
  b. Through threats, implied or expressed, that relief would be cut or denied, unless the client voted right?
  c. By "helping" the client get to the polls to vote?
  d. By showing special favors to outspoken clients of the party in office?

(7) What kinds of pressure were exerted to decrease relief expenditures?

    a. By the newspapers?
    b. By opposition political parties?
    c. By organized interest groups such as the Liberty League?
    d. By advocating direct relief in preference to more expensive work relief?
    e. By advocating the return of relief to state and local communities?

2. Changes in relative importance of the taxing units:
    (1) Trend in the proportion of relief financed by municipalities?
    (2) Trend in proportion of relief financed by townships and towns?
    (3) Trend in proportion of relief financed by counties?
    (4) Trend in proportion of relief financed by states?
    (5) Trend in proportion of relief financed by the federal government?

3. Changes in the amount of bond issues and the kinds of taxes used to finance relief:
    (1) Trends in the amount of bond issues in:
        a. Cities?
        b. Townships and towns?
        c. Counties?
        d. States?
        e. Paper of the federal government?
    (2) Trends in the proportion of relief financed out of:
        a. General property taxes?
        b. Taxes on intangibles?
        c. Net income taxes?
        d. Inheritance taxes?
        e. Gross income taxes?
        f. Excise taxes?
        g. Sales taxes?
        h. Head taxes?
        i. Corporation taxes?

4. Effect of experience with relief upon attitudes toward laws of legal settlement:
   (1) What proportion of clients had no legal settlement?
      a. Individual transients?
      b. Individual homeless residents?
      c. Transient families?
      d. Homeless resident families?
   (2) What special problems arose and what temporary solutions were found in states with long-residence requirements?
      a. In early years of the depression?
      b. During the federal period?
      c. In the post-federal period?
      d. Was there a difference in problems arising out of direct relief and work relief?
   (3) What special problems arose and what temporary solutions were found in states with short or no residence requirements?
      a. In early years of the depression?
      b. During the federal period?
      c. In the post-federal period?
      d. Was there a difference in problems arising out of direct relief and work relief?
   (4) What amendments have been made to state laws regarding legal settlement as a result of the relief experience?
      a. In states with long-residence requirements?
      b. In states with short or no residence requirements?
5. Effects of public relief policies upon private social agencies:
   (1) What has been the trend of contributions to community chests during the depression?
      a. With respect to larger contributions?
      b. With respect to moderate contributions?
      c. With respect to employees' contributions?
      d. With respect to total contributions?

(2) Have changes in emphasis among types of private social agencies occurred, which are reflected in budgets?
  a. Trends in private relief budgets?
  b. Trends in private institutional budgets?
  c. Trends in "character-building" agency budgets?
  d. Trends in private health agency budgets?
(3) What changes have occurred in the relations of private social agencies and public welfare agencies?
  a. As to proportion of relief costs borne?
  b. As to the division of labor between the two types of agencies?
  c. As to a sharper definition of the functions of the private agencies?
  d. As to comparable qualifications of personnel?
6. Increased interest in leisure-time problems:
(1) Increase in number and size of parks and playgrounds?
  a. Constructed out of regular local governmental funds?
  b. Constructed out of work relief funds?
(2) Increase in use of public buildings for recreational and other leisure-time purposes?
  a. School buildings?
  b. Park buildings?
  c. Library buildings?
(3) Growth in variety of facilities for leisure-time activities?
  a. Playground equipment?
  b. Park accommodations, such as swimming pools and playing fields?
  c. Leaders provided out of work relief funds?
(4) Larger participation in adult education?
  a. Classes in reading and writing?
  b. Other classes?

    c. Vocational education?

    d. Informal groups?

    e. Use of library suggestions for reading?

(5) Does there appear to have been an acceptance on a wider scale of the theory that a constructive use of leisure time is a proper concern of government?

    a. As reflected in recreational budgets of governmental units as federal funds declined?

    b. As reflected in better personnel in public recreational departments?

    c. As reflected in the expansion of public libraries and the establishment of more accessible branches?

4. NOTE ON METHOD

A number of small studies have been made of several of the problems suggested above, but a comprehensive study of the whole problem of the effects of relief policies upon community organization is contemplated in the foregoing outline. An example of how one angle of the problem may be approached is afforded by a study recently made by Anita Wells of the Works Progress Administration, entitled *The Distribution of State and Federal Relief Funds among the Political Subdivisions of the States.* The actual proportion of relief costs which was paid by each level of government was presumed, by the authorities concerned, to be upon the basis of need. The research problem was not alone to determine the proportions paid by each level of government in different states, but also to examine the methods for "the measurement of need" which were used in each state. One general practice was to have the local relief administration submit estimates of budgetary needs each month for the subsequent month, and then the state administration deducted from this estimate the amount payable from local funds, leaving the remainder to be paid by state and federal funds. Sometimes the basis of allocation of grants-in-aid was population or population plus previous expenditures. Some state allocations were made upon the basis of the percentage of the local population which was estimated to be unemployed. The final decision as to how much the local governmental unit could pay was based upon some guessing and some political maneuvering. At one time Illinois used a sort of "index of local effort" by which those counties which had paid a high percentage of their own relief costs received relatively large grants of federal funds and smaller loans from the state bond issue, whereas counties which had paid relatively small amounts of their own relief costs were given small grants from federal funds and larger loans from state funds. The result was monthly variations in allocation ratios. At various times Ohio used three factors for determining allotments: population, previous expenditures, and local assessed valuation. Some states allocated state and federal funds on a percentage, or matching basis. In Rhode Island this method resulted in the local governmental units paying six-elevenths of the total cost and the state paying five-elevenths, but a special fund was held in reserve from which additional grants were made to financially distressed localities. Consequently, the determination of the actual percentages of relief costs paid by local, state and federal governmental units would have to be made from a study of the records of expenditures.

What is proposed in the foregoing outline is a study of trends in percentages of payments made by the different levels of government. The WPA study gives samples of the allocation of funds, determined by a more or less rule-of-thumb "measurement of need," but it would be more useful for future development of policies to determine whether or not experience during the depression has led to any tendency toward a uniform standard for the "measurement of need" of grants-in-aid.

Chapter X

Social Effects of Work Relief Policies

WORK relief during the current depression has been planned and carried out on a larger scale than in any previous business depression. In previous periods of great economic distress it was sporadic and local; in this one it began with limited local programs but in 1933 became national in scope.

1. POLICIES

In the early years of the depression a few work relief projects, supported by community chests and certain public agencies, were conducted experimentally, and a considerable number of local public relief authorities adopted the policy of requiring work for food baskets or grocery orders. The Wicks Act in New York State, adopted before the Federal Emergency Relief Act, provided state aid for work relief projects. Beginning in 1930 public opinion seems to have begun to develop in favor of work relief in contrast to direct relief. It was asserted that the recipient of work relief was better able to maintain his self-respect than the recipient of direct relief, and it was widely believed that to require a certain amount of work for public assistance would automatically weed out the malingerers. Against this background of experiment and discussion the gigantic work relief programs of the Federal Emergency Relief Administration have been organized and administered. The Federal Act, passed May 12, 1933, provided that the Administrator might make grants to the states "to aid in meeting the costs of furnishing relief and work relief." The Administrator assumed office May 22, 1933, and on May 23 notified all governors that federal funds would be granted in the ratio of one dollar of federal money to three dollars expended "out of public moneys from all sources." As a matter of fact, however, the ratio was never put into effect in many states. It was optional with the states to use the money for direct relief or work relief. If work relief was used, the "rate of wages should be a fair rate of pay for the work performed," but under any circumstances the amount of wages should equal, but not exceed, the "budgetary requirement of the relief recipient." The one-to-three ratio did not last long; soon the federal government was paying the major cost of relief in all states.

Work relief projects under all the work programs had to be in connection with federal, state or local public property. The projects were required to be independent of regular public works under contract or for which an annual appropriation was made. They were expected to be apart from normal governmental enterprises and, as such, would not have been carried out in normal times. Projects were subject to approval by the state emergency relief administrations.

The great national work relief programs began with the creation of the Civil Works Administration on November 9, 1933 (Executive Order 6420-B). Previous work programs had been piecemeal by comparison with this one. The aim was to put to work immediately four million unemployed persons, one half of whom were taken from relief rolls. The state CWA approved projects under rules prescribed by the FCWA. Wage scales based on degree of skill required and geographical zone were established. For various reasons the FCWA was terminated March 31, 1934, and in its place was set up the Emergency Work Relief Program of the FERA. Under this program a stricter means test was inaugurated to determine eligibility of individuals for employment on projects. The applicant must have been on the relief rolls or eligible for relief under the rules of the FERA. Projects were still approved by the state ERA's. This program continued until the spring of 1935 at which time orders went out to the states to liquidate the direct relief and the work relief programs of the FERA. On May 6, 1935, the Works Progress Administration and a new works program were created (Executive Order 7034). The aim of this new program was to employ by December, 1935, 3,500,000 persons who had been on relief rolls between May 1 and November 1, 1935. State administrators were designated, very often the same persons who had been in charge of the state ERA's, but they were responsible to Washington for their activities. The WPA has been continuously under direct federal administration. All projects were approved in Washington. Wage scales, based upon degree of skill and geographical area, were fixed. The professed intention of the Works Progress Administration was to take all employable persons from the relief rolls, give them work under the new program and leave the so-called unemployables to be carried on direct relief by the states. However, a considerable number of employable persons was never given work under WPA because of the limited funds and the inability to find enough acceptable projects.

2. PROBLEMS

What have been the social effects of these work relief programs which have cost several billion dollars? Differences of opinion concerning the answer to this question have resulted in sharp controversy. It is important, both to give a factual basis for these opinions and to provide some guidance for future relief policies, that an effort be made to answer this question.

It has been the contention of those who favor work relief rather than direct relief that work relief keeps the morale of the unemployed at a higher level than direct relief. The individual on work relief is able to maintain more nearly a normal, everyday life pattern than the individual on direct relief: he leaves his home during the day, he has a job, he returns home after work, he receives wages, and he and members of his family may spend the money as they see fit. Local work relief programs very often did not provide for paying wages in cash, but in grocery orders or even food baskets. In any attempt to evaluate the contribution to morale of work relief the method of payment is important; it is highly probable that wages paid in grocery orders or food baskets had much less favorable effects on morale than did cash wages, because this kind of work relief resembles closely the old "workhouse test." Some of the more subtle effects on morale may be connected with the worker's feeling about the particular job to which he was assigned. Was it a real job that needed to be done, or was it just made-work? Many persons closely associated with the work programs believe that the morale value of work relief depends a great deal upon the worker's estimate of the usefulness of the project upon which he is working.

The method of certification for a works project is probably also important. Under local programs relief status, with possibly some attention to the number of dependents, was the criterion. When the CWA came into existence, certification was done by the United States Employment Service, and for half of those employed by the program proof of unemployment was sufficient to get certification. Under the works programs of FERA and WPA certification depended upon relief status, but the USES was better organized than under CWA to do relatively good placement, and this effort to determine what kind of job a client could do may have contributed something to his morale. The methods of certification and placement furnish a part of the data for the study of morale.

Many projects directly contributed to better morale. One special group of work relief projects of this type should be mentioned, and that is the great variety of recreation projects. These projects gave work relief employment to large numbers of clients, and they provided opportunities for many more members of relief families, especially children. The more adequate provision of recreational facilities may have had an effect upon juvenile delinquency in some localities.

Another matter closely related to morale is the comparative adequacy of subsistence provided by work relief and direct relief. Under the "workhouse test" variety of work relief there was likely to be very little difference in the dollar value of the amount received, but under the federal programs there was, at least in some localities, a considerable difference in favor of work relief. The important question is: how much more did the client on work relief receive than he would have received on a direct relief budget? The answer is not as simple as it may seem, because the consumption requirements of a working man are greater than those of one who is not working. He must have a higher caloric content in his diet, and he may have to buy additional clothes. The changes in budgetary items under work relief, upon which allowable earnings were based, require examination, after which the cost of these items can be compared with earnings. The wage scales specified in federal rules and regulations are an incomplete guide, because in many localities, especially in the southern states, these wage scales were adjusted to local conceptions of what relief should be. To the wages received must, of course, be added the values of surplus commodities distributed to the family.

The assignment of individuals to particular jobs, as suggested above, affected morale, but it also affected wages received and efficiency on the job. In the early works programs the methods of selection of workers for jobs were rather crude, but during the federal period the methods approached nearer to the standards of good public employment service. Beginning in 1933, and perhaps in a few states before this date, the USES handled assignments in a manner as nearly as possible like their regular procedure, but sometimes the volume of work was so great that it was done hurriedly. Nevertheless, in the files of the offices of the United States Employment Service and in the offices of the regular affiliated state employment services there are records which give at least the client's statements of his previous work history. It is doubtful that work references were checked very thoroughly as a guide to specific placement in a job. Many complaints were made that skilled workers were assigned to ordinary manual labor; this may have been due to the speed with which work assignments were made or to the relative scarcity of skilled jobs. In 1933, 1934 and the early part of 1935, opportunities for skilled workers on work relief projects were fairly plentiful, and skilled workers were available, but when private employment began to show a steady increase in the latter part of 1935 and in 1936, skilled workers were rapidly absorbed into private employment. This created a shortage of skilled workers on work relief projects and necessitated the assignment of unskilled persons to jobs for which they had little or no previous experience. Consequently, there are two problems here: to what extent were skilled workers assigned to unskilled jobs and to what extent were unskilled workers assigned to skilled jobs? Another question bearing upon these two problems was the extent to which the needs of a family rather than occupational fitness determined the assignment to a given work relief project. This did enter into a decision at times, because the relief worker assumed that the net earnings from work relief would provide a higher level of subsistence than the same family could get on direct relief. Such assignments may have been sufficient in number to reduce the efficiency of some work relief projects.

Little thought was given to vocational training on the job in 1933 and 1934, and it is doubtful that any was given during the pre-federal period. But in 1935 and 1936, when skilled workers for relief projects became scarce, some effort was made to train workers for skilled occupations. The extent to which apprenticeship training for young persons and retraining for older workers were given will be difficult to determine, because they depended largely upon the interest and ingenuity of the local project supervisor. Vocational training was not a systematic plan which was pushed by the federal administration, although it was encouraged. In so far as the client was given a job which was suitable for him, work relief tended to preserve old skills and the neuro-muscular coordination necessary for occupational success. If, as a matter of fact, persons employed on work relief projects were able to find jobs in private employment sooner than those who were always on direct relief, this does not prove that work relief gave them vocational training or preserved old skills, because it is not impossible that a selective process went on in the relief administration which resulted in the selection of the better class of unemployed for work relief assignments. The extent to which work relief contributed to vocational training and to maintenance of old skills will be difficult to measure, but it is of the first importance in the consideration of future work relief policies.

Soon after the beginning of CWA "public works of art" projects and projects for actors and writers began to appear. This is probably the first time in the history of the country that the United States Government appears in the rôle of patron of the fine arts on a grand scale. This novelty in relief administration has its partisans and its severe critics; the term "boondoggling" may have been applied to leaf-raking first, but it has perhaps been applied more often to fine arts projects. To the relief administration, which was attempting to find projects suited to the previous occupational experience of relief clients, it seemed just as logical to set up fine arts projects for unemployed artists as to set up construction projects for unemployed engineers. A determination of the contribution which the relief administration has made to the fine arts will be as difficult to make as the determination of the morale value of work relief in general, but it is an important matter in the cultural life of the country and is unquestionably a social effect of relief policies. These projects did give employment to artists in their usual occupations which doubtless contributed to their morale and gave them some incentive to do good work under depression conditions. Quantitative studies will be very limited; they can show the number of painters, sculptors, actors and writers who were employed and for how long, and perhaps they can show the number of unit artistic productions. The quality of artistic production can be determined only by the usual methods of art criticism, but it would be highly desirable to have a competent study made of the quality of the artistic productions done under the relief administration.

In the very nature of the case, work relief projects had to be concerned with public property or with activities, devoid of private profit, which were "affected with a public interest." Many of the projects were in the nature of "public works" or closely allied to public works. In the pre-federal period municipal authorities are known to have discharged regular garbage collectors and to have presented garbage collection as a suitable work relief project, but such crude substitutions of work relief projects for ordinary municipal obligations and such contributions toward swelling the number of the unemployed did not last long. The federal rules and regulations prohibited any relief project which would take the place of regularly budgeted public works, but such a policy was hard to enforce, not merely because local officials tried to evade it, but also because it was actually difficult to determine whether or not a piece of public construction would have been postponed indefinitely if there had been no work relief program. The problem for investigation here is not so much to determine to what extent local governmental authorities shifted their costs to the federal government but rather to determine how nearly the normal volume of regular public works was maintained during the depression because of work relief projects. Such projects included street maintenance and construction, road maintenance and construction, erection of public buildings, development of parks and boulevards, con-

struction of levees, repairs on public buildings, additional workers in public offices, social surveys, etc., etc. These projects were
all set up by some municipal, county, state or federal governmental agency which had a regular budget. The budgets for
years preceding the work relief programs are matters of record,
and the costs of relief projects in wages and materials are matters of record. From these records a fairly definite answer can
be given to the question: what has been the trend of expenditures in municipal, county, state and federal public works budgets, separating regular appropriations and relief expenditures
so as to determine them separately and then together?

The object of the answer to this question is not to convict
local governmental authorities of evading their plain duties but
to determine how the public welfare has been served by means
of work relief expenditures. The communities have gained
something in permanent values from the completed work relief
projects, and these gains should be determined. It is a complex
problem: (1) a large number of clients had their morale bol-
stered up because of work at real wages, which is one of the
imponderables; (2) the purchasing power of the relief group
was raised in terms of dollars which meant an increase in retail
business; (3) money spent for materials meant business for
the durable goods industry; (4) the difference between work
relief wages and what the direct relief outlay would have been,
plus the cost of materials and some supervision, is the excess
cost of work relief as compared with direct relief; (5) the community has a net gain in capital assets and in relatively un-
measurable service. How much have these items cost in relief
funds and what is the net material gain to the community? Along
with this inventory of capital assets should go, of course, a consideration of the extent to which regular employees were displaced by relief workers; some cases are known where regular
employees were laid off and then taken back in their old jobs
as relief workers. How successful was the relief administration

in preventing the substitution of relief workers for regular employees in local governmental projects?

Somewhat related to the foregoing problem is the percentage of normal working efficiency which was achieved on work relief projects. Uncritical estimates have ranged all the way from twenty-five per cent to one hundred per cent efficiency with most of them ranging from about sixty to eighty per cent. The Governor's Commission on Unemployment Relief in New York estimated that "The efficiency of operation maintained upon the projects examined by the representatives of the Commission was found to be, on the average, at a level of 74.8 per cent of what might be expected to prevail upon like ventures under average contract prosecution" (Report to Governor Herbert H. Lehman, 1936). Since the creation of the Works Progress Administration, probably a more systematic effort has been made to determine unit costs than prevailed in the other work relief programs. On engineering projects the costs of wages, material, equipment, supervision and other items have been determined and then the unit cost per cubic foot, cubic yard, square foot or lineal foot has been determined. Many projects, of course, do not lend themselves to computation of unit costs in terms of cubic feet, etc., and the strictly service costs probably cannot be reduced to units under any circumstances, but those projects dealing with materials do offer the possibility of determining the ratio of labor costs to material costs and then comparing the unit cost with the unit cost of similar work under the usual contract arrangements. Also the man-hours (because of the terms in which projects are often described it may be necessary to use man-months) required to use a given amount of material on work relief projects can be compared with similar work done under contract; this is a better measure of efficiency than unit cost, if "prevailing wages" were not paid on work relief projects.

One of the less discussed social effects of work relief has been the effects of work relief projects upon the values of adjacent private property. It has been no obligation of relief administrators to undertake this kind of computation, but in appraising the value of work relief to the community in general it is of great importance. Many miles of levees have been constructed along rivers and creeks which overflow in times of heavy rains. Some of the land adjacent to such rivers and creeks is highly desirable for farming or for residence purposes in cities, and the construction of a good levee has had the immediate effect of raising the price of this property and sometimes of stimulating the construction of houses. The construction of roads, especially feeders for main highways, has made farms more accessible to markets. Many miles of streets have been paved or repaved, and sometimes this has occurred without the usual assessment upon property owners, which means that they profited at least to the amount of the uncollected assessment. Much work has been done to improve sanitation in and around cities; some of these projects have doubtless tended to enhance private property values. Boulevards have been extended beyond city limits into the open country—sometimes through hills and along beautiful creeks—one result of which has been to increase suburban home construction near these extensions. Less tangible but nevertheless a fact, are the effects which state park and state forest work had upon nearby real estate. Records of property which was sold before and after the works projects in the locations suggested above are available to consult in efforts to measure the effects of work relief projects upon adjacent private property. When we attempt to determine what work relief has cost the country, in comparison with direct relief, it is reasonable to consider the enhancement of private property values, along with capital gains in public property, as in a sense credits against the cost of work relief.

One aspect of the work relief policy has not yet been discussed, and that is the pressure for speed in the organization and submission of projects. There was very little of this in the pre-federal period, perhaps none, but from the day of the announcement of the CWA until the present time pressure for speed has been ever present. Charges have been made by those who disapprove of work relief and also by those who do approve of work relief as a policy that the demand for speed has resulted in many poorly planned projects and in a consequent waste of money, not to mention the effects upon the morale of the workers. Some useful projects were doubtless rejected by federal supervisors who could not possibly know the value of all projects submitted and, hence, rejected those which seemed queer or collided with their prejudices. Some study should be made of the results of hasty organization and approval or disapproval of projects. The problem is rather intangible, and probably no satisfactory quantitative appraisal can be made, but a competent analysis of the problem and the judgment of the analyst would be valuable for future developments of relief policies.

3. RESEARCH PROBLEMS

The problems indicated above have wide ramifications, and the task of assembling the data for their study will be great. But the practical importance of the problems will probably justify any amount of time and money that is expended. The following outline suggests some of the specific questions which research should attempt to answer:

1. What morale values does work relief have and how important are they?
    (1) Does working for food baskets (the "workhouse test") have morale value?
        a. When the amount of relief is the same as the client received without working?
        b. When the food basket is supplemented with some additional relief in kind?
        c. What kind of work was done by the client?

(2) How did certification for employment under CWA affect morale?
    a. Did the fact that the client had to register with the Employment Service have a good effect?
    b. How important for morale was the fact that half of the workers were not on relief but just unemployed?
    c. Did clients like employment in this first large work relief program?

(3) Have the morale values of work relief been greater or less under the FERA and the WPA respectively?
    a. How important in relation to morale was the fact that relief status was necessary for certification?
    b. Have clients sought work relief in order to get off direct relief?
    c. What changes occurred in the month-to-month waiting list, members of which were seeking work relief jobs?
    d. Has the demand for work relief jobs been more marked under WPA than under FERA? Why?

(4) What contributions have recreation projects made to morale?
    a. What kinds of recreation have been offered?
    b. What has been the attendance of client families at recreational activities?
    c. How much client participation was there in recreational activities?
    d. Have the recreational projects been located so that they were convenient to large numbers of clients?
    e. What evidences exist to show what the recreation policy of the relief administration contributed to the morale of clients and their families?
    f. Have recreation projects, especially park projects, contributed to the morale of others than clients? How and how much?

2. Was the standard of subsistence provided by work relief higher than that of direct relief?
   (1) In terms of dollars?
       a. Wages received?
       b. Surplus commodities in addition to wages?
   (2) Were consumption requirements on work relief higher for the same level of living than on direct relief?
       a. Did the worker require more food in order to work?
       b. Did the worker have to buy extra clothes?
       c. How much did work relief raise the level of living of families?
   (3) What changes occurred in the budgetary items when a client changed from direct to work relief?
       a. Qualitative?
       b. Quantitative?
3. How were clients selected for work relief projects?
   (1) What was known about the work history of the client?
       a. Did the U. S. Employment Service, the FERA Work Division and the WPA Division of Employment have any history other than the client's own statement?
       b. Did these placement offices follow up references?
       c. What was known about the health of the client?
       d. What, if any, occupational tests were used?
   (2) What was the extent of placement because of fitness for the particular job?
       a. Were there enough skilled jobs for all skilled workers under CWA?
       b. When did the supply of skilled workers begin to be scarce for work relief projects?
       c. Did skilled workers who found private employment and left skilled work relief jobs get skilled jobs in private employment?

     d. What percentage of skilled workers were given unskilled jobs?

     e. What percentage of unskilled workers were given skilled jobs for which they had little ability?

     f. How much did the various placement officers know about the requirements of a job when they referred a client?

(3) What effects on the skilled worker were noticeable, if he had to take an unskilled job?

     a. Did he complain?

     b. Was there evidence of malingering to escape from such jobs?

     c. Did it affect his morale badly?

(4) To what extent was the need of the family the basis of certification for work relief instead of occupational fitness, when a selection had to be made?

     a. Was this a policy of local relief offices?

     b. If fitness was the basis of assignment, how did the employment service go about locating the right client?

     c. When assignments were to be made did the machinery for cooperation work smoothly between:

       (a) The USES, the CWA and the ERA?

       (b) The USES, the Social Service Division and the Work Division?

       (c) The relief agency, the WPA, the USES and other federal agencies?

4. Was there a systematic effort to do vocational training by work relief officials?

(1) How much apprenticeship training on the job was attempted for young persons?

     a. Did they understand that they were being taught to do a job?

  b. Did the foreman take time to teach his apprentice?

  c. For what trades was training given?

  d. How many individuals received definite training?

 (2) Was there any effort to retrain older workers?

  a. In new trades?

  b. For their former occupations on which they may have become "rusty"?

  c. How many older workers were retrained?

  d. For what occupations was retraining undertaken?

 (3) What were the results of efforts at vocational training?

  a. Did relief workers want it?

  b. How many of them were enabled to find jobs of the sort for which they were trained?

5. What has been the contribution of work relief to the fine arts?

 (1) What have been the values of painting projects?

  a. What proportion of this work has been recognized by competent critics as technically good?

  b. What has been the public contribution made by murals?

  c. What was the age distribution of painters on the projects?

  d. Have the projects helped young painters in particular?

  e. What has been the attendance at exhibits of paintings by work relief artists?

  f. Have the painters had freedom to work out their own conceptions? What became of their work?

 (2) What has been the contribution of sculpture projects?

  a. How much competent work has been done?

  b. How many sculptors worked on these projects?

  c. What was the age distribution of the workers?

  d. What has been the attitude of young sculptors

toward the opportunity offered them on relief work projects?

e. Have sculptors had freedom to work out their own conceptions?

f. What has become of their work?

g. How much public interest has been shown in these projects?

(3) What has been the value of the work relief theatre?

   a. How many professional actors have been given employment?

   b. How many amateurs have participated as actors?

   c. What kinds of plays have been presented?

   d. Who selected the plays?

   e. What do competent critics think of the work relief theatre? Its quality and educational value?

   f. What has been the attendance at performances?

   g. What plays have had the best reception? Why?

   h. Were costumes and stage properties made by clients?

(4) What has been the contribution of the writers' projects in terms of creative writing?

   a. What creditable fiction has been produced?

   b. What creditable poetry has been written?

   c. What plays have been written?

     (a) How many have been produced by the commercial theatre or the motion picture industry?

     (b) How many have been produced by the work relief theatre?

     (c) What have been the dominant ideas of the plays?

   d. What is the estimate placed upon these literary productions by competent critics?

   e. Has the writing represented realism, romanticism or classicism?

6. Has work relief made possible approximately the normal volume of local public works?
   (1) What was the trend of various municipal, county and state public works budgets during the depression?
      a. For the fiscal year ending in 1933?
      b. After the opening of the new fiscal year in 1933?
      c. Were necessary services, such as sanitation and street repairs, curtailed?
   (2) How much was spent for corresponding public works out of relief funds?
      a. Before the federal period?
      b. During the federal period?
      c. Did the regular budget plus the relief budget for work relief projects show an increase in the volume of local public works?
      d. Have work relief funds made possible a balanced public works program?
   (3) To what extent were regular employees displaced by work relief employees?
      a. When the federal work relief program got under way, was there a tendency for local governmental units to reduce their own appropriations more?
      b. To what extent were regular employees discharged and then taken back in their old positions as work relief employees? In schools and offices?
      c. Were promises of economy in local governmental expenditures by candidates carried out, while public works were maintained at a normal or better level by work relief funds?
      d. What departments of local government capitalized the work relief opportunities most?
      e. How much of the work done by work relief employees was substitution for necessary public works and how much was supplementation?

(4) What is the permanent value to the community of completed work relief projects?

   a. How much street repair and construction was done with relief labor?

   b. How much road repair and construction were done with relief labor?

   c. How much sewer work was done with relief labor?

   d. How much work was done on public buildings with relief labor?

   e. How much work was done on publicly owned public utilities with relief labor?

   f. How much park and playground work was done with relief labor?

   g. How much work was done on publicly owned transportation systems with relief labor?

   h. How much work was done on dams, levees, breakwaters, beaches, piers, etc., with relief labor?

7. What kinds and how much surveying and research were done with the help of work relief funds?

(1) How much of the work of state planning boards has been done with relief labor?

   a. Topographical surveys?

   b. Soil surveys?

   c. Studies of transportation problems?

   d. Studies of industrial problems?

   e. Studies of residential housing?

   f. Planning of public building construction?

   g. City planning?

(2) What studies of local and state government have been undertaken with the help of relief labor? How much and what kind of relief labor?

   a. How much technical and professional help was paid from relief funds?

    b. How much clerical help was paid out of relief funds?

    c. What was the contribution of relief labor to these projects?

(3) What was accomplished by national research projects set up to be conducted mainly with relief funds?

    a. The parole study project?

    b. The study of technological factors in unemployment?

    c. The study of problems related to social security?

    d. The health study?

(4) What has been the value of special research projects conducted by members of university faculties but with a large amount of relief labor:

    a. Sociological projects?

    b. Projects relating mainly to economics?

    c. Projects relating mainly to political science?

    d. Social service projects?

    e. Projects dealing mainly with psychological problems?

    f. Projects conducted by biologists?

    g. Projects conducted by physicists?

    h. Projects conducted by chemists?

    i. Projects conducted by geologists?

    j. Projects conducted in other scientific fields?

(5) What has been learned about the value of continuous research in the field of social service for administrative purposes from the fact that the Federal Emergency Relief Administration has had from the beginning a Division of Research?

    a. Have the studies which were made provided a valid scientific basis for the development of relief administration?

    b. Has it been worth the cost to do the numerous small sample studies which have been made?

c. As the work relief programs have developed, have we learned much about:
   (a) The kind of research that can be done by an administrative agency?
   (b) The kind of research which is technically useful to the agency?
   (c) The validity of studies based upon small samples?
   (d) To what extent were the official investigations carried on chiefly for publicity purposes?

8. What has been the degree of efficiency of relief labor?
   (1) What has been the degree of efficiency maintained:
      a. On street and road construction?
      b. On repair and construction of public buildings?
      c. On other construction work?
      d. On regular office work?
      e. On projects requiring technical and professional knowledge and skill?
   (2) If the degree of normal efficiency is low, is it attributable to:
      a. The methods of selection for assignment to work relief projects?
      b. Lack of interest on the part of the workers?
      c. Ineffective supervision by foremen?
      d. Shortage or inadequacy of materials?
      e. Rapid turnover of the labor force?
      f. The physical condition of the workers?

9. What effects have work relief projects had upon the values of adjacent private property?
   (1) What values have been added to real estate because of the construction of levees:
      a. In cities?
      b. In rural communities?
   (2) What values have been added to private property:
      a. By the construction of roads, especially feeders?

    b. By street construction?

    c. By the improvement of sanitary or swamp conditions?

(3) When street work was done as relief projects:

    a. Did property owners on the street pay a share of the cost?

    b. Were the usual assessments made by the city on owners of adjacent business or residential property?

    c. When such work was done on streets which had street car lines, did the street railway company pay a part of the cost?

(4) What was the effect on real estate values of boulevard extensions with relief labor?

    a. Did the price of land rise?

    b. Was suburban construction stimulated?

    c. Was the market for adjacent property more active?

(5) What were the effects of park and forest work upon the values of adjacent real estate?

10. What were the effects of federal pressure to set up projects quickly?

(1) Did this result in approval of poorly planned projects?

    a. Because of the mass production idea back of federal policy?

    b. Because the project inspectors must of necessity know more about some kinds of work than others?

    c. Because of the influence of local politicians?

    d. What percentage of projects may be regarded as in a large measure failures from the viewpoint of work accomplished?

(2) Did this result in the rejection of some good proposed projects:

    a. Because the inspector of projects did not understand them?

    b. Because the field representative did not understand them?

    c. Because the inspector or field representative was prejudiced against a proposed supervisor of a new project?

(3) Did this result in improving the morale of the unemployed and the community:

    a. Because it was evidence of the sincere interest of the federal government in doing something about unemployment?

    b. Because it meant fast movement which had the psychological effect of convincing people that progress was being made?

    c. Because the unemployed gained the feeling that the government was working night and day to take them off direct relief and give them jobs?

4. NOTE ON METHOD

The foregoing outline suggests the wide ramifications of a research plan whose purpose is to make an appraisal of the social consequences of the work relief policies. A number of sample studies have been made dealing with some of the subjects indicated above, and one of the best of these is contained in *Work Relief in the State of New York, A Review of Its Characteristics, Functioning, and Value,* by the Governor's Commission on Unemployment Relief, submitted to Governor Lehman August 10, 1936. This study attempted among other things to determine "The Value of Work Relief to the Communities." The Commission found that $124,266,696.95 had been expended in New York state for 201,788,520 man-hours of work. After an inspection of 599 projects the Commission concluded that 95.5 per cent of them were worthwhile, 85.9 per cent had definite survival value, 96.8 per cent were in line with the development of the communities, and 90.1 were provided with competent plans and designs. Only 4.8 per cent of the finished work was poor, and 23.0 per cent was very good. Operating efficiency was on the average at a level of 74.8 per cent. The methods of arriving at these percentages are not given, but they appear to be based upon impressions rather than measurement. In a sample of white-collar projects studied by the Commission the conclusion was drawn that 68 per cent were good, 31 per cent fair and 1 per cent poor; from the viewpoint of efficiency the projects were rated as follows: 43 per cent good, 45 per cent fair and 12 per cent poor. A "composite rating" of the comparative worth of projects, considering the "purpose and results, efficiency in operation, and contributions actually made to the public and to the workers," indicated that 42 per cent were excellent, 31 per cent good, 23 per cent fair and 4 per cent poor. The Commission believes, "despite the restrictions of subjectivity and of flexibility in bases for evaluation," that its judgment is fairly accurate. While agreeing that work relief makes useful contributions to the community, the Commission is very skeptical of the net economic advantage of it, "because (a) the displacement of regular employees renders many of them destitute, eventually, (b) the efficiency is, on the whole, lower than that of the regular employees, and (c) since prevailing hourly wages are paid, the sum total cost of carrying on an unchanged amount of governmental services cannot be reduced by utilizing relief workers." This study, like some others contained in the report, represents careful impressionistic estimates of work relief, but from a scientific viewpoint it lacks precision. Qualitative, relatively indefinable terms, such as "excellent" and "fair," are used. It is believed that, if efficiency were measured in terms of productivity per man-hour or on construction projects in terms of cubic feet or square feet, or some other definable unit, a more convincing appraisal could be made. Many of the subjects indicated for investigation clearly do not lend themselves to measurement, but, on the other hand, a considerable number do, and in the study of the latter, quantitative methods should be used.

Chapter XI

Effects of Relief Policies upon the Labor Market

RELIEF policies have affected the organization and the processes of the labor market, both because they have affected
the incentives of individuals to seek private employment, and
later, were related to the public employment service. The amount
of relief granted in the early years of the depression was so small
in most localities that it would not have encouraged individuals
to prefer relief to wages for work, but the fact that it was so
low may have damaged the physical capacity for work and produced despondency. Later the amount of relief was more nearly
adequate for subsistence, and under some circumstances work
relief may have had attractions superior to those of private employment. Wages in some localities seem to have been affected
by the amount of direct relief allowances and wage rates for
work relief projects. All of these things are related to the fluidity
of the labor market.

1. POLICIES

From 1930 to 1936 the inclination has been to think of relief
as an emergency measure, the need for which would soon disappear, and the clients would soon find work in private industry. Relief policies were directed partly toward the organization of the labor market through the public employment services
and partly toward providing incentives for seeking work, although their primary objective was to assure the provision of
subsistence for families and individuals without income. The

existence of such objectives or relief policies creates the starting point for extensive research. The problem for research might be stated in the form of a question: How and to what extent did relief policies affect the employment or re-employment of clients in private industry either by facilitating it or by retarding it? It was possible to formulate relief policies which would assure minimum subsistence to unemployed persons but which failed to provide the incentive and the machinery for the gradual re-absorption of clients in private employment. In the early part of the depression well implemented policies for re-absorbing unemployed persons in private employment were lacking in most states. In 1933 the United States Employment Service was strengthened by the passage of the Wagner-Peyser Act, and out of funds provided by the Federal Emergency Relief Act the Federal Re-employment Service was financed for the purpose of supplementing the regular employment service. These two services were closely coordinated with the administration of relief, the result of which was to improve greatly the machinery for putting clients back into private employment, but the provision of incentives to seek private employment was more difficult. Specific relief policies had to be defined and made flexible so that opportunities for re-employment would be attractive. The attractiveness of a job depended partly upon the wages offered and the urge to self-maintenance, but it was in no small degree conditioned by the physical vitality of the unemployed person which might have been seriously damaged by a destitute level of living imposed by low standards of material relief.

2. PROBLEMS

The aim of the present public employment service is to organize the labor market as completely as possible. The degree of success attained will depend to a large extent upon expert selection of individuals for reference to an employer. The service will have the respect and confidence of both employers and workers only if it understands the technical requirements of the job which is open and the technical abilities of the individual who is referred for the job. The private employment agencies have built their limited achievements upon the foundation of good placements, but theirs was a small enterprise operated for profit and in competition with one another, whereas the public employment service proposes to organize the entire labor market in the interest of the public welfare. Its task is immensely greater than that of the private employment agencies, but its success, no less than theirs, will turn upon expert placement.

It is a common opinion among relief workers, admitted by some officials of the employment services, that many referrals have been made on the basis of need rather than upon the basis of qualifications for the vacant job. There are several explanations of this, such as pressure from relief agencies to get jobs for certain individuals whose families were in need of more income than the relief budget would permit, pressure from relief administrators to take clients off relief and put them into private employment, and pressure from politicians to get jobs for their friends in order to cement their support. However laudable some of these referrals may have been from the viewpoint of human sympathy, they were in contravention of the basic principle of good employment service and tended to destroy respect for the competency of the employment service. When unemployed persons begin to draw unemployment compensation benefits, there may be the same inclination to find jobs for the recipients of benefits, regardless of qualifications for the jobs available, in order to relieve pressure on the reserve funds. As a basis for estimating the possible extent of such pressure in the future it would be well to know how many of the referrals during the depression have been made on other grounds than technical qualifications. An efficient public employment service has much to contribute to national per capita production.

The public employment service has been more important during this than in any former depression. An active attempt has been made, not merely to urge clients to seek work, but to find jobs for them. The relation of the public employment service to the re-employment of clients is an important subject for study. After the beginning of the Works Progress Administration clients were directed systematically to register with the local employment office, and penalties were prescribed for failure to register, but prior to this time, except for a brief period under CWA, registration seems to have been less general. Registration, however, was not all that was required: the client was often notified of a job in private employment and was required to take it, if he was acceptable to the employer. Most clients probably accepted every such opportunity, but there were some who needed external incentives. We do not know how many failed to report to the employer, after being notified of a vacancy, or what action was taken by the employment service or the relief agency. The client might be anxious for employment and report to an employer but fail to get the job. Perhaps he did not have the qualifications for the job, but in some localities employers seem to have discriminated against the client who had been out of work for a long time, and it is possible that age, sex, race and nationality were grounds for discrimination against some clients. It is to be expected that an employer would take the applicant who seemed best fitted for the job, but the factors which determined eligibility for employment should be studied. One of the conditions which is not clearly understood is the apparent fact that industrial production has risen much more rapidly than industrial employment has risen or than unemployment has declined. Several millions of young people are now competitors for jobs, but they do not sufficiently account for the entire lag in employment or maintenance of unemployment. The relations of the relief agency and the employment service to this problem might be studied, although in general, this problem appears to be one inherent in the present industrial setup rather than one susceptible to influence by the relief agency.

Throughout the depression there has been a large amount of temporary employment available. A client might take a temporary job, earn for a short time somewhat more than his relief budget, build up his morale in some degree and free the relief budget from payments to him for the duration of his employment. But when such an opportunity came to a client, if he were removed from the relief rolls and would have to be reinvestigated before having his case reopened, he would hesitate to accept the job. Reinvestigation in some localities, at least, was slow, and there is some feeling that this lag caused distress. Temporary employment might also offer the client opportunity to earn somewhat more than he needed at once for the subsistence budget. This would permit him to buy much needed clothes for members of the family or possibly to pay an installment on old debts. However, if the relief agency insisted that he budget his earnings in the same terms as his relief budget and spread his income over a period of time equal to the time for using the same amount of relief money, the client had much less incentive to look for and to accept a temporary job. On the other hand, if the client were encouraged to take temporary work with the explicit understanding that he could use his own judgment about spending his earnings and that, while his case would be suspended, it would not be closed, a definite incentive would be given to take temporary employment.

Part-time employment differs somewhat from temporary employment. It may be regular or irregular, but in either case the wages amount to less than wages for full-time work. During the depression, as at other times, there was a great deal of part-time employment available. Some part-time employment might yield wages equal to or in excess of the relief budget, but much of it was less than the amount the client had been getting from the relief agency. In localities where the relief policies permitted the agency to make part-time work attractive to the client, the result may have been a stimulation of the morale of the client and a slight decrease in the amount of relief given. If the agency allowed the client to have a somewhat larger budget, as recognition of his efforts to find work, it provided an economic incentive to the client to seek other part-time work. Some agencies report that they allowed clients to retain their regular relief allowance and at the same time to earn small sums at odd jobs. A study of a group of such cases in several localities might throw light upon methods of providing incentives to self-maintenance.

A factor closely related to the problem of re-employment is the minimum wage scales on work relief. Relief wages were undoubtedly higher in some places than wages of unskilled labor in certain kinds of private employment. Complaints have been made that certain employers have taken advantage of the large number of persons on relief and available for work to reduce wages to a point lower than either direct relief or work relief wages. On the other hand, it has been reported that, where work relief wages were about the same as wages in private employment, the client has preferred to "work for the government" and has refused private employment. Some of the large work relief projects have had clients in relatively important positions and have probably been reluctant to have them leave for private employment, although the federal policy required the release of such a person with the understanding that he would retain certification for work relief. The United States Employment Service has been an important part of this re-employment machinery and has been under the obligation to refer clients to private employment, regardless of their value to a work relief project, and it would be interesting to know how many times they have been requested by supervisors of projects to pass over certain men and find some one elsewhere for referral.

Experience has shown that the reabsorption of unskilled workers in private employment has been slower than the reabsorption of skilled workers. Many of the skilled trades ceased to take apprentices, or reduced the number taken. Industries which formerly trained many young people for semiskilled jobs have taken fewer. The result seems to be a shortage of workers in a number of important skilled occupations. Some effort has been made on certain work relief projects to convert unskilled workers into skilled workers. A certain amount of training-on-the-job has been done. The employment service has been in a strategic position to know the demands for various skilled occupations, but whether or not the relief agencies were informed of the demands in various skilled-work occupations is not clear, nor is it certain that their efforts at training had any relation to the demands. This problem has very great public importance.

3. RESEARCH PROBLEMS

The following outline suggests in some detail the approach to the problems indicated above:

1. If a client took a temporary job, was it easy for him to get back on relief when the job was finished?
   (1) Procedure for readmission to relief rolls:
      a. Was there a definite waiting period after the job ended?
      b. Was reinvestigation required in all such cases?
      c. How much time elapsed between reapplication and the first relief payment?
   (2) Encouragement to take temporary work through:
      a. Explicit understanding that client could return to relief rolls?
      b. Allowance of a somewhat larger budget?
      c. Permission to use some of earnings to buy clothes for members of the family?
      d. Permission to pay installments on old debts?
      e. Permission to use earnings without restriction or checkup by the agency?
2. Incentives to accept part-time employment:
   (1) Policy with respect to regular part-time work:

    a. Did the agency supplement earnings to make up the deficiency in the budget?

    b. Did the agency allow an increased total budget?

    c. How many clients had part-time employment?

    d. How long did part-time employment on the average last?

    e. Did part-time employment result in a saving to the agency?

(2) Policy with respect to occasional part-time work:

    a. Was the amount of earnings from odd jobs subtracted from the agency allowance?

    b. In how many cases was the client allowed openly to keep his earnings and still receive his usual relief allowance?

    c. Where one agency reduced the budget by the amount of earnings, and another did not, what was the difference in the number of clients reporting part-time work?

3. How much, if any, did the minimum wages and wage rates for work relief projects affect the reabsorption of clients in private employment?

(1) With respect to unskilled labor:

    a. Were rates higher than prevailing wage rates in private employment?

    b. Did the setting of relatively high minima tend to raise wage rates in private employment?

    c. Did relief policies operate to depress wage rates in private employment because the employer thought the client would like any amount he could get over and above work relief wages?

(2) With respect to skilled labor:

    a. To what extent were prevailing rates paid?

    b. If prevailing rates were not paid, how much less were work relief rates than private rates?

    c. Where prevailing rates were paid, was there a preference for work relief employment?

(3) The importance of security of tenure and certification under WPA:

    a. Was security at a slightly lower weekly income preferred to less security with higher weekly income in private employment?

    b. Was the degree of security of continuous employment on WPA exaggerated?

4. The extent of vocational training and retraining:

(1) What kind of training was offered?

    a. Special classes?

    b. Training-on-the-job?

    c. For what types of skilled or semiskilled work?

(2) What were the vocational characteristics of clients who were given vocational training?

    a. Age distribution?

    b. Sex distribution?

    c. Per cent being retrained for old occupation?

    d. Per cent being retrained for new occupation?

    e. What specific handicaps did trainees have?

(3) Relation of training for given vocations to demands for persons with such training?

    a. What information did the employment office supply as to demand for specific types of skilled and semiskilled workers?

    b. Did relief agencies, which undertook to do training, work out their plans on the basis of known demand for certain kinds of workers?

5. Referral of individuals to jobs by the public employment service on the basis of need rather than upon the basis of qualifications for the job:

(1) Was pressure exerted to get the employment offices to refer certain individuals for jobs by:

    a. Local relief agencies?
    b. Relief administrators?
    c. Politicians?
(2) Distribution of referrals of clients by degree of success on the job:
    a. How many received the jobs for which they were referred?
    b. How many failed to secure the jobs for which they were referred?
    c. How many received the jobs but were released for inefficiency?
    d. What was the average length of time various kinds of jobs lasted?
(3) Preference given to clients with dependents:
    a. When qualifications of clients with and without dependents were apparently the same?
    b. When qualifications of clients without dependents appeared to be better than those with dependents?

6. To what extent did the relief agencies see to it that clients registered with the U. S. Employment Service prior to and after the inception of the WPA?
(1) Did clients refuse employment when called by the employment office:
    a. Because they preferred direct relief or work relief?
    b. Because the conditions of work would be unreasonably bad?
    c. Because they were unqualified for the jobs?
(2) Among those registered did the employment office note any discrimination on the part of employers because of:
    a. Age?
    b. Sex?
    c. Race?
    d. Nationality?

(3) Effect of length of relief period upon re-employment:

   a. Was it easier to place clients who had been on relief a short time?

   b. Why were clients who had been on relief a long time discriminated against by employers?

(4) What proportion of clients received their jobs through employment service?

   a. Was the rate of re-employment higher in states with an organized employment service than it was in states without one?

   b. Was there any important difference in the length of time jobs lasted for clients in states with and without the United States Employment Service?

7. What contribution did relief policies make toward the development of the public employment service?

(1) In the pre-federal period:

   a. By occasional referral of clients to local employment offices?

   b. By obtaining additional funds for the employment service?

(2) In the federal and post-federal periods:

   a. By systematic referral of clients on both direct relief and work relief?

   b. By familiarizing a large number of people with the employment service, when they had to register?

   c. How many clients registered with the employment service?

4. NOTE ON METHOD

The difficulties in the way of answering some of the questions above are obvious. Some of them can be answered rather definitely by statistical methods, but others are non-quantitative and depend for answers upon other kinds of analysis.

An illustration of how one of the complex questions, namely, the extent of refusing jobs, may be given an approximate answer will be given here. The Division of Research of the WPA has made several local studies of alleged "job refusals." One of these dealt with 262 relief clients in Buffalo, New York. These clients were alleged to have refused jobs in May and June, 1935 (see WPA Research Bulletin, Series I, No. 15).[1] For the purposes of this study "job refusal" was taken to include cases in which the individual had not only refused a specific job, but had failed to answer a notice of a job which was sent to him by the New York State Employment Service. The 262 cases were chosen from a list of 457 charged with job refusal, but upon preliminary investigation of the relief records it was found that 195 either were not on relief rolls at the time the job was offered or were not actual May or June refusals of nonrelief jobs. After these were eliminated from the study, the records of the New York State Employment Service and the Buffalo Emergency Relief Bureau were analyzed to secure all available data regarding the offers of jobs and the reasons for refusals. Supplementary information was obtained from interviews with the clients and with the employers who were reported to have offered the jobs. Miscellaneous interviews were arranged with a number of persons representing a variety of interests in the city. As a result of the study, it was found that 8 individuals refused private employment because they preferred relief or work relief, 56 claimed physical disability although they were registered with the Employment Service as available for work, and 42 claimed that they had failed to receive the notice of the job. Of the 56 claiming disability, 22 furnished evidence of disability, but the remaining 34 could not give evidence of good faith for refusals on this ground. Of the 42 cases of alleged failure to receive notices, 17 sub-

---

[1] This study is perhaps not representative of the various studies made, because a larger percentage of genuine refusals were discovered among the alleged refusals than in any other study.

stantiated the claim, but the other 25 could not present proof of failure to receive notice. Altogether the reasons for alleged refusal to accept private employment amount to 16, and the number of individuals falling in each class is indicated. The conclusion drawn is that there were apparently unwarranted refusals of private employment and that the Emergency Relief Bureau bears some of the responsibility in these cases for inefficient execution of the re-employment policy of the WPA.

This summary shows that some of the factors involved can be determined on a fairly objective basis, such as illness or employment elsewhere at the time the notice was sent, but others involve wide margins of personal judgment. Many sources of information were used, but the most important sources were the Employment Service and the Emergency Relief Bureau. Much the same technical problems, suggested in this illustrative case, will be found in the attempt to answer any of the questions proposed under this project.

Chapter XII

Some Economic Effects of Relief Policies

THE aim of relief policies to preserve life and maintain physical health has a direct economic implication, because the preservation of working capacity is the result. Relief policies however seem to have had a number of other economic effects.

1. POLICIES

Outside of expenditures upon the regular governmental establishments, "government spending"—federal, state and local— has been directly or indirectly for relief purposes throughout the depression, but since early in 1933 the budgets have been larger and the economic effects more noticeable. In former depressions in this country and in the pre-federal period of this depression, relief has been given mainly for humanitarian reasons; it was to relieve the suffering of the unemployed. That has been no less an aim in the administration of relief since the Federal Emergency Relief Act, but it was supplemented with the theory that relief on a scale adequate to maintain health would also contribute toward the recovery of normal economic activities which would reduce unemployment. The moderately inflationary viewpoint of the New Deal replaced the deflationary viewpoint of the previous national administration as a way of coping with unemployment in both its humanitarian and its economic aspects; the policy of stimulating consumption by putting purchasing power into the hands of the unemployed in order to stimulate demand supplemented the policy of loans to industry as a means of increasing employment. It is the economic effects of this innovation in American relief policy, introduced by the New Deal, which require comprehensive, factual analysis on a scale not yet undertaken.

The policy of organizing work relief and public works on a large scale seems to have had important effects upon both public and private economics. Support of self-help cooperatives and the attempt to establish cooperative communities has been a special activity in the work relief policy, but it may have given the cooperative movement in this country an impetus which it had not previously possessed. Federal grants-in-aid to the states for relief purposes were on a larger scale than any former grants-in-aid, and this method has been followed by the states with reference to local governmental units. By the incorporation of grants-in-aid in the Social Security Act and in the recent public welfare legislation of the states this method of financing various types of relief has become permanent. This development may have an important influence upon the smaller political subdivisions as administrative and taxing units.

The immediate, and very difficult, problem of the research worker who attempts to determine the economic effects of relief policies is the identification and isolation of those expenditures which occurred because of relief policies. Under the New Deal, relief administration was an integral part of the effort to hasten industrial recovery. From a long-range viewpoint perhaps no dichotomy should be made, because the New Deal did think of relief as a positive tool as well as a means of immediately reducing the amount of suffering, but in order to understand relief and to plan future relief policies, it is desirable to attempt the dichotomy and to try to measure the economic effects of relief expenditures.

2. PROBLEMS

What have been the effects of relief policies upon the purchasing power of the recipients of relief? Presumably those among the unemployed who were not on the relief rolls still had either money or credit with which to purchase the means of subsistence; this is not wholly true, because relatives and friends often helped. It is assumed that those receiving relief had little or no other means of subsistence. In the pre-federal period the percentage of normal purchasing power which a relief allowance provided was small, but it was something. The case records for this period are meager in many states, but probably there are enough available in some states to determine in some degree the ratio of usual earnings to relief allowances. It would be instructive to distinguish between the percentage of purchasing power maintained for clients on work relief and for those on direct relief in the early years of the depression (some localities, and New York State in particular, had a fairly large volume of work relief).

During the federal period there have been three levels of relief purchasing power throughout the country: direct relief, work relief and public works. The amount which a client received, and hence the percentage of his normal purchasing power which was maintained, depended upon which kind of assistance he had. Average receipts from direct relief were smallest, next above those were wages from work relief and highest of all were wages from employment on public works. There has been an inclination in some quarters to deny that employment on public works was relief, but, if a public works project was financed out of relief funds, it was certainly relief for all those who had been on the relief rolls and had simply transferred to a public works job. Some of the employees on work relief projects were drawn from among the unemployed who had not asked for relief, and possibly some of them had left private employment to take public works employment. If a distinction can be made between relief clients and nonrelief clients engaged upon public works, it is desirable that a study of the relief aspects of public works should be made. The usual wages in private employment will be given in the case record ordinarily. It is the practice of the Works Progress Administration to get some data on previous occupational history of all workers, and earnings history may be available for some. The Public Works Administration does not keep such records in its own files, but the contractor who was given the job of carrying out the project would keep his own personnel records which, at least in the case of large projects, would undoubtedly contain information regarding occupation and earnings.

A related, but perhaps more involved, problem is the extent to which the retail price level was affected by the large relief expenditures. The answer to this question would require isolation of the effects of relief expenditures from the effects of the NRA, AAA and the gold policies of the federal government, but it might be done with respect to particular commodities which enter largely into retail trade. When the FERA got fully under way, relief budgets of families rose considerably; more food, clothing and the like were purchased. The government took over large quantities of agricultural commodities which were distributed to clients as "surplus commodities." The increased resources of clients and the purchase of surplus commodities undoubtedly created a stronger demand for farm products, and it is possible that this increased effective demand, especially after the crop curtailment program had begun to take effect, stimulated prices.

The effects of relief policies upon retail business, if important, were due to the increased purchasing power of clients, but it would be desirable to describe these in terms of retail business. Considerable information, such as department store sales, is available, and monthly, if not weekly, relief expenditures during the federal period are known. Correlation analysis should be a means of determining the degree of relationship between relief expenditures and the volume of retail business. The CWA period presents almost a controlled experiment for a study of this problem. We do know that retail sales during December, 1933, were higher than they had been for some time, and we know that a short recession from recovery began in the spring of 1934, after the CWA was discontinued and relief funds were spent at a slower pace. The WPA provided another experiment for a similar study. Some commodities or some kinds of stores may have responded more than others to increased relief expenditures. Comparisons among a number of states would be interesting, because the relief allowances and work relief wages varied by states, and they varied between urban and rural areas. When relief was a small matter of local charity or pauper relief, its economic effects could be neglected. But it has been big business since the spring of 1933, and its consequences for retail business are of great importance.[1]

This problem is seen in its true perspective when relief is considered from the viewpoint of its effects upon general economic recovery. Giving the consumer the purchasing power to remove goods from the shelves of retail stores, as a means of removing other goods from the shelves of wholesalers and of increasing the demand for factory output, was at the heart of the New Deal theory of a planned recovery. Those who believed in spending as the way to recovery were in favor of large appropriations for relief. There was a difference of opinion concerning the manner in which relief should be given, and the result has been a compromise by which three forms of relief have been in existence throughout the depression, although work relief and public works became larger proportions of the total program than they had been prior to 1933.

The analysis of the relation of the relief program to recovery breaks down into several problems, one of which is the extent to which the methods of financing relief stimulated or retarded

---

[1] For a more detailed discussion of consumers' expenditures see Vaile, Roland S. *Research Memorandum on Social Aspects of Consumption in the Depression.* (monograph in this series)

recovery. Funds for local relief costs were derived partly from taxes and partly from sale of bonds. State grants-in-aid were financed in the same ways. Tax rates to pay relief costs rose. Bonds were sold both to banks and to the general public, or rather, they were sold through banks to the public. The federal government did not raise enough money from the usual sources to pay the costs of the regular establishment, in spite of certain additions to the excise tax list; consequently, it borrowed from banks and gave its obligations. Before 1933 the administration theory was that as much of relief costs as possible should be paid out of taxes and that borrowing should be reduced to the lowest possible minimum; this was the pay-as-you-go theory. Under the New Deal the theory of relief finance was to keep taxes as low as possible and borrow what was needed. With reference to recovery there are two problems here, both of which require more study than there has been time to give them up to the present: first, to determine whether or not it is best for the public welfare to reduce taxes as low as possible and then to borrow for relief purposes, and, second, to determine, if resort is had to borrowing, whether bonds or other obligations should be sold to the general public or absorbed entirely by the banks.

A considerable proportion of relief funds was spent for materials to be used on work relief projects and public works.[2] That necessitated some rather large orders to the heavy industries: steel, cement, sand and gravel, lumber, machine tools, copper, etc. The number employed and the amount of the payrolls in these industries were influenced by these orders for materials to carry out relief projects. The operation of these industries on higher schedules led to increased activity in transportation and various kinds of service. The additions to employment and the larger payrolls increased the demands upon

---

[2] See current numbers of the *Monthly Labor Review* for expenditures for certain classes of materials.

the entertainment industries. At least, these are the events which, according to the New Deal theory, occurred. Since relief funds were large, the effects should have been appreciable. The problem for research is to determine what these alleged effects were and how important they were. The aggregate amounts spent on all materials can be determined from the project records, but the amounts spent for different kinds of materials will have to be determined partly from records of work relief projects and partly from the records of contractors who carried out the public works projects. Purchase orders will indicate the particular firms from which materials were purchased, and their records contain production and personnel data.

Another problem of some importance is the alleged competition of private business and government undertakings for skilled labor. Late in 1935 complaints began to appear that certain kinds of skilled labor were hard to find; public employment offices reported that they could not fill all of the requests which were coming from employers. It was about that time that the WPA was approaching maximum employment and that some of the largest PWA projects were under construction. Did these projects require any of the categories of skilled labor which were said to be too short for the requirements of private industry? It was the explicit policy of the WPA to release any worker whose services were needed by a private employer, but a public works project was different. While the funds for it came out of the relief appropriation, the actual work was awarded to a contractor on the basis of competitive bidding, and he was probably under no obligation to release his skilled workers to a competitor who might be constructing a factory building or an apartment house. Regardless of any legal or ethical obligations involved, the facts in this situation should be studied.

A problem of longer range than recovery is conservation of natural resources and the effects which relief policies have had upon it. The National Resources Board and the affiliated state planning boards have been financed for most of their lives out of relief funds, and one of their chief problems was to study methods of conservation and more efficient methods of utilization of natural resources. Theirs has been a long-range planning job; it has not been the administration of conservation projects. But hundreds of projects related to conservation have been carried on by various governmental units. A report was made early in 1936 that more than 100,000,000 trees had been planted by workers who were paid out of relief funds. Reforestation has been accompanied by a large amount of work to reduce fire hazards. Existing state and national forests have been enlarged, and new lands have been bought for forest purposes. Flood control projects have been authorized in almost all states. Some of these projects have consisted of the construction of log dams in creeks, but others have resulted in the construction of miles of levees on river banks and huge dams to create water power and reservoirs. The CCC and some of the transient camps have in the aggregate done a great deal of soil erosion work, although by comparison with what needs to be done it may be only a good start. Nevertheless, much useful work has been done. A study of this work and an estimate of the potential public and commercial wealth which has been created should be made. An appraisal of the accomplishments of the relief program will be incomplete without such a survey.

Relief policies have had some effects upon the cooperative movement. For the most part this influence has been exercised in the direction of producers' cooperatives. The relation to these is clear, but the effects upon consumer cooperation are less certain. The *Handbook of Consumers' Cooperatives in California* lists eighty-five "self-help cooperatives" whose object was some kind of production and which were financed in part by relief funds. Service, such as that provided by this *Handbook,* has helped to organize information and means of communication for those interested in cooperatives, and it is mainly a handbook for consumers' cooperatives, although relief funds have apparently not entered into the consumers' activities. Relief funds, however, have been available in limited amounts in a number of states to aid the self-help producers' cooperatives, and the agencies handling rural relief have attempted to establish new agricultural-industrial communities in which the emphasis appears to have been on production but was accompanied by consumers' organization. Farm cooperatives were involved in the collection of surplus commodities for delivery to the relief administration; the importance of this fact depends upon the value to the farmer of this market for his produce. It would be useful to determine the number and kinds of cooperatives which were assisted by relief funds, the amount of business they did, the number of members they had and what specifically was the contribution of the relief administration to their success or failure. Another matter which cannot be measured but which is important is the amount of publicity which attended the establishment and development of the agricultural-industrial communities; this may have added greatly to the support of the cooperative movement, and, if it did, the result is a consequence of a relief policy.

The effects of relief policies upon organized labor have probably been considerable, but the nature and importance of these effects remain to be determined. Many union members were unemployed and had difficulties keeping up even nominal dues. In the pre-federal period it is doubtful that relief amounted to enough in many localities to permit any expenditures for dues, but this may have been possible during the federal period for those on direct relief in some localities, and it was certainly possible for all those on work relief or public works. The relatively large relief allowances or relief wages in the federal period probably kept the union treasuries in a much stronger position than they otherwise would have been during the depression; without considerable funds they could not have carried on the campaign for organization of the heavy industries and for the election of their candidates to public office.

A more direct way of aiding organized labor by means of relief was to provide relief for those who were on strike. Because this could be done and was not uncommon, the strikers were able to hold out longer; they had the financial support of their unions, and they had the relatively unlimited provision of subsistence by the relief administration. This situation gave organized labor much the same kind of strong position which it has in a time of booming industrial activity when the demand for workers is great. Furthermore, a union worker who happened to be employed on a work relief project did not have to accept an offer of private employment, if its acceptance would conflict with the standards of work established by his union; he could refuse the job and remain on the work relief project.

A complicated situation arose when there was a strike of workers on a relief project: on the housing projects of the PWA these strikes were often jurisdictional, but on WPA projects they were often directed at the sponsor of the project. It would be interesting to know whether or not strikers on a WPA project received direct relief and, if so, how extensive this was. There was close cooperation of work relief and public works administrators with the unions; the administrators generally left the initiative for the designation of their members for a project to the union. In the case of public works, members of a union on relief had to be certified first, but after this supply was exhausted the union might certify any of its members. The union was thus an active agent in both placement and spreading work among its members; this undoubtedly instilled in the minds of the members a growing respect for the effectiveness of the union.

One influence seems to have worked at cross-purposes with organized labor, and that was the fact that the relief wage scale in some localities was deliberately placed a little lower than the union scale for similar work and that in all localities the total amount of weekly wages was less than it would have been for full-time work at private employment. Employers may have taken advantage of the fact that maximum monthly wages on work relief were a relatively small fixed amount and attempted to cut the wages of a weak union. The subject of the effect of work relief wages or public works wages on union wage scales is of great importance in connection with the maintenance of purchasing power of consumers, and a thorough study of it should be undertaken.

On the side of public economics, the subsidies and grants-in-aid by federal and state governments have probably had important effects. In practice a subsidy is usually understood to mean financial assistance to a subordinate governmental unit by a superior governmental unit but not in a fixed ratio to funds provided by the subordinate unit; and a grant-in-aid usually means financial assistance to a subordinate governmental unit in some predetermined ratio to the total funds used. Subsidies have generally been more elastic than grants-in-aid, which means that political influence is a more important consideration in fixing the amount of the subsidy to a particular governmental unit. The FERA began with a proposition to provide one dollar to every three dollars spent by the state and local governments, but in less than a year the differences in degree of economic distress existing in the states and in the amount of political influence had resulted in wide variations in the proportion of relief costs which the federal government was paying. For the most part the distribution of PWA funds was in the form of loans and grants-in-aid; the grant-in-aid was a definite percentage of the cost of the project, and individuals with influence could not easily get this percentage altered in their favor.

The grant-in-aid and the subsidy principles were incorporated into the Social Security Act, but the aggregate amounts of grants-in-aid appear to be much larger than the subsidies. Hence, these principles have now become permanent in the relief and social security programs of the federal government, and the new state public welfare laws which are being adopted have utilized especially the grant-in-aid principle. This type of financial participation in the welfare program by superior governmental units may result in more adequate support for welfare work, but it may mean reduced financial support by the local governmental unit. By some it is feared that grants-in-aid and subsidies will produce a deeper entrenchment of outworn local administrative agencies, which will spend the larger public funds just as inefficiently as they have spent their local funds in the past. On the other hand, the state or the federal government which provides a subsidy or a grant-in-aid for local use is likely to insist upon the right of inspection and of some degree of supervision as a condition of financial support; this means a reduction in the relative importance of the local unit and a gradual integration of the whole system from the local unit to the federal government. Regardless of what happens in the long run, the effects will be registered in public finance, in the manner and in the amounts of income and outgo. Relief policies to some extent in the pre-federal period influenced this development, but the vast sums of money given as subsidies and grants-in-aid by the federal government under the New Deal created a pattern which, as shown by the Social Security Act, has become a permanent and more important part of our governmental organization.

3. NOTE ON RESEARCH PROBLEMS

The foregoing comments upon the economic aspects of the relief problem will suffice to indicate the magnitude and the complexity of the relations of the relief program to economic organization and economic functions. No attempt has been made to suggest all of the possible economic aspects of relief policies. Any adequate study of this phase of the relief problem would require a research plan in which economists would play perhaps the largest part, but political scientists and sociologists would have an important part in it. The persons qualified to study the economic effects of relief policies would probably want to state the problems differently, but the writers have tried to call attention to some of the problems which seem important to those who have had some contact with the various relief administrations.

Because the subject of this chapter differs sharply from the subjects of the other chapters and because of its wide ramifications, it has seemed best not to outline specific projects for research, as was done in the other chapters. A better list of projects could perhaps be made by a committee representing administrators and representatives of several social sciences.

Chapter XIII

Effects of Relief Policies upon the Qualifications of Personnel

DURING the pre-federal period public relief in most states was administered by workers whose only qualification for the job was political eligibility; a few states and municipalities are exceptions to this general situation. In a great majority of states the "overseer of the poor" was an elective official who appointed whatever staff he wanted, which had whatever qualifications he thought necessary. The personnel policies of the Federal Emergency Relief Administration, in so far as the states were concerned, were hortatory rather than mandatory. However, the suggestions of the federal government had more than ordinary weight, because the states needed funds for relief and were under the necessity of establishing standards of administrations which were reasonably satisfactory to the FERA.

1. POLICIES

In Rules and Regulations No. 3, issued July 11, 1933, the federal government mentioned personnel qualifications: each local relief administration should have at least one trained and experienced investigator on its staff; there should be not less than one supervisor, trained and experienced in the essential elements of family case work and relief administration, to supervise the work of not more than 20 investigating staff workers. Investigation of all applications for relief was required, but the FERA could not "require" personnel qualifications. Under CWA the intention was to carry on this work with existing personnel, but provision was made for the appointment of "ad-

147

ditional technical personnel" by the federal administrator. Notice was sent to all state administrators May 15, 1934, that the FERA would allocate funds to the states for the training of social workers during the summer and through the next year. Plans for the emergency education program sent out in June, 1934, provided for the selection of supervisors in cooperation with the state superintendent of public instruction, which indicated a requirement of some standards for supervisors. In a communication from the federal administrator August 15, 1934, regarding partisan politics it was stated that "continued employment of personnel must be on the basis of qualification." The stipulations regarding personnel qualifications were meager and very general, and refer specifically only to social workers and only indirectly to supervisors of the emergency educational program. Apparently no definite personnel standards were established for the selection of administrators, assistant administrators, technical employees, accountants, statisticians and clerical workers. Of course, after the federal government withdrew from direct relief the state and local administrations were entirely free to select whomever they wished by whatever standards they set up, if any. But the instructions and orders relating to the establishment of the Works Progress Administration contain no direct references to qualifications of personnel.

In view of the fact that qualifications for personnel under all relief administrations during the depression were either lacking or indefinite, it is all the more important to study the qualifications which regular employees of the relief administrations actually had and to consider carefully the methods which were in fact used for the selection of personnel. Furthermore, it is insufficient to study the qualifications of case workers and case work supervisors only. These workers have had the limelight, but the complexity of the organization of the vast relief administrations has placed ultimate responsibility for achievement upon the state administrator in most cases, and he has had to have a small army of assistants, technical staff and clerical workers to keep the organization going. The qualifications of all of these workers have a bearing upon the efficiency of administration, and it is necessary to study all of the personnel policies to determine their consequences.

Attention should be called to the fact that in some cities, and perhaps elsewhere, clients were used as "investigators." That is, they took the place of qualified professional personnel. The effects of this practice upon morale and efficiency should be included in a plan for the study of the effects of relief policies upon qualifications of personnel.

2. PROBLEMS

The administrative machinery for the selection of personnel needs to be determined. In some of the large offices there was a supervisor of personnel whose duty it was to receive applications, to interview applicants and to refer them to the departments where vacancies existed. Many supervisors and subexecutives located their own personnel and then referred them to the personnel office, if any, for routine checkup. In local offices, unless the appointive power was held by the state office or the federal administration, the executive probably handled the employment of personnel. Application forms which contained various information about applicants were in general use and have been kept on file. Access to these for research purposes could probably be obtained. Before the federal period and after the withdrawal of the federal government from direct relief, the entire responsibility for handling personnel was in the hands of local officials in many states. To determine the actual organization in local communities may require understanding the relation of the relief official to the local political organization. Notwithstanding federal instructions to the contrary, political influence also probably played its part in federal and state appointments, which means that the methods of selecting personnel involve the political organization. If political endorsements were necessary to get appointments or if they influenced some appointments, a realistic study of personnel organization must give these facts their correct weight.

What kind of people did the personnel organization succeed in getting into the relief administration? Evaluation of the organization itself is perhaps less tangible than an appraisal of the qualifications of the persons who were actually given appointments. The age and sex of workers appears on the application for a position. Age is particularly important, because some of the sharpest criticism of the administration of relief centered around the youthfulness of some of the workers. In the pre-federal period academic and professional qualifications were given slight attention in most states, but during the federal period standards for case work personnel were set up which were believed to be as high as possible, considering the relatively small number of persons in the country who had good educational qualifications for social work. Not a great deal was heard about the qualifications of other personnel, but probably standards for accountants, statisticians and clerical workers could have been set at a reasonably high level. The experience and educational qualifications of executives and subexecutives are perhaps more varied than those of any other group. Some of them came from the field of professional social service, but many of them had never been employed by a social agency. Some of those without previous social service experience did distinguished work. One of the most important and thus far baffling problems in personnel research is to find some method by which executive ability can be described and identified. The amount of academic education, the kind and amount of professional or vocational education and the kind and amount of previous employed experience can generally be ascertained from the application forms and other personnel records, though these records are less likely to give full information about executives. Qualifications of personnel should be examined with reference to the degree of success attained in the relief administration; some insight into this problem might be gained from a study of complaints, transfers and dismissals.

Another important problem is the determination of the proportion of employees engaged in the several activities of relief administration. If a state administration was giving direct relief to 100,000 cases, how many assistant administrators, how many supervisors, how many case workers, how many technical people, how many accountants and how many clerical workers were used? What differences appear in an organization handling a similar number of work relief cases? What seems to be a proper balance in types of personnel for maximum efficiency? Were the relief policies concerning personnel such as to attain a balanced personnel organization? These are questions of the first importance for future policies of relief administration, and the data available for their study are fairly plentiful. There were forty-eight state relief administrations, and there were many hundreds of county organizations. Some criteria exist for comparing the relative efficiency of administrative units, such as promptness of investigation and making a decision after an application for relief has been received—records sufficiently complete to give an understanding of the current status of relief families, delays in dictating interviews, the ratio of complaints of clients to total case load, etc. Some relief administrations ran more smoothly than others, and it is important to know how important a relatively balanced personnel organization was in this connection.

As the relief problem grew in magnitude during the depression, the need for some kind of training for workers who were entering the administration became pressing. In the pre-federal years some efforts were made in this direction. They consisted mainly of short institutes for local workers and a few instances of more systematic training. The federal program made possible more serious attention to training. A great many experienced workers were pulled out of private social agencies and put into the national relief organization. These experienced workers, in so far as personnel existed and politics would permit, put trained persons in supervisory positions who attempted to give some training on the job to "case aides" and other new case work employees. Conferences and institutes continued to be widely used for some ad hoc training, not only for case workers but for sub-executives. By 1934 a plan of cooperation between the FERA, the American Association of Social Workers and the American Association of Schools of Social Work had been worked out. The FERA made funds available to the state administrations for training purposes. A certain number of new workers with a sufficient amount of general education, some of whom had not started to work, were sent to accredited schools of social work for a semester or two quarters at the expense of the government. These federal students took the regular classroom and field work courses offered by the schools, and at the end of their period of training returned to the states which sent them. In some states, through state universities or in some other way, a qualified instructor in social case work gave courses, some of which carried university credit, to social workers in the field. This was a continuation of the plan of training-on-the-job but in a more systematic way. Some study of this many-sided training program of the FERA should be made to determine the number of relief workers who received one or more of the various kinds of training and the value which it had for relief administration. Alongside of this study might profitably be placed a study of the quality of work done by social workers who previously had had a year or more at one of the accredited schools of social work. To bring together all of such available information and carefully analyze it would be useful, not only to future policies regarding personnel, but to the schools of social work to which increasing numbers of students are going.

The third major stage in the personnel problem began when the federal government withdrew from direct relief in 1935. In many states the responsibility for direct relief reverted to the local elected overseers of the poor who proceeded to reorganize the relief staff. In some localities trained workers were anathema to these officials, though in states which had some central control the degradation of personnel qualifications may not have gone so far. But even in those localities where there was either political objection or popular prejudice, or both, against the professional social workers, some of the trained workers were retained. An instructive study could be made of the comparative qualifications of case work personnel in the pre-federal period, the federal period and the post-federal period in direct relief. Where direct relief was in the hands of elected officials after the withdrawal of the federal government, personnel records may be more difficult to obtain for research purposes, but probably enough can be secured to make such a comparative study worthwhile.

3. RESEARCH PROBLEMS

The following outline is proposed as an approach to the various studies of personnel which may be made:

1. How were employees for the administration of relief selected?
    (1) In the pre-federal period?
        a. What organization existed for selecting personnel of all kinds?
        b. In municipalities and counties?
        c. In states where a state relief administration was set up?
    (2) In the federal period?
        a. Did the federal government attempt to give direction to a personnel policy?
        b. What was the state personnel organization?
        c. Did local administrations control the selection of personnel for their agencies, or did the state have

some initiative or veto power over local personnel?

(3) In the period after the federal government withdrew from direct relief?

 a. How many states continued to exercise some control over local personnel?

 b. In how many states did local authorities have complete control?

 c. How much initiative in the appointment of work relief personnel did the states have?

 d. Did the WPA have to approve all appointments or only certain grades?

2. What kinds of persons were actually appointed to relief positions in the three administrative periods?

(1) What was the age and sex distribution of employees in such positions as the following:

 a. Executives and subexecutives?

 b. Case work supervisors?

 c. Case workers?

 d. Technical staff?

 e. Accountants?

 f. Clerical workers?

(2) What was the academic education of the following types of employees:

 a. Executives and subexecutives

 b. Case work supervisors?

 c. Case workers?

 d. Technical staff?

(3) What was the professional or vocational training of employees appointed to the following positions:

 a. Executives and subexecutives?

 b. Case work supervisors?

 c. Case workers?

 d. Technical staff?

 e. Accountants?

    f. Stenographers?

    g. Filing clerks?

(4) What experience in work similar to that required under the appointment had the following employees had?

    a. Executives and subexecutives?

    b. Case work supervisors?

    c. Case workers?

    d. Technical staff?

    e. Accountants?

    f. Clerical workers?

3. What percentage of the total personnel in a relief organization had such positions as the following in the three administrative periods?

    (1) Executives and subexecutives?

    (2) Case work supervisors?

    (3) Case workers?

    (4) Technical staff?

    (5) Accountants?

    (6) Stenographers?

    (7) Filing clerks?

    (8) Other clerical workers?

4. What was done about training social work personnel after they were given appointments during the three administrative periods?

    (1) What kind of training-on-the-job was undertaken?

        a. Was it a limited case load under an experienced supervisor for a certain period?

        b. Were there night classes conducted by members of the staff?

        c. Were there classes in case work conducted by a qualified instructor from an accredited school of social work or employed by the relief administration for this purpose?

    d. To what extent were local, regional and state conferences used?

    e. To what extent were institutes used?

    f. How much effort was made to get untrained workers to read the literature of professional social work?

(2) What was the nature of, and how important were cooperative relations with, professional social work organizations, such as:

    a. Local chapters of the American Association of Social Workers?

    b. The national organization of the American Association of Social Workers?

    c. The Joint Vocational Bureau?

    d. The American Association of Schools of Social Work?

(3) What was the experience with scholarships to send employed workers to accredited schools of social work?

    a. How many workers attended such schools on FERA scholarships?

    b. What was the age and sex distribution of these students?

    c. Did these workers make an important contribution to local relief administration when they returned?

    d. How did they compare with others who had already in the recent past had a year or more at a school of social work?

    e. How many of these students later returned to schools of social work for further professional education?

5. What were the qualifications of social workers after the federal government withdrew from direct relief?

(1) What percentage of the old workers were kept by local relief authorities?

(2) How were appointments made?
(3) What were the qualifications of the workers?
(4) What were the qualifications of the executives?

4. NOTE ON METHOD

Some limited studies have been made of relief personnel, but no comprehensive national study has been published. One of the short studies was made in 1934 by the Federal Emergency Relief Administration and published under the title of *Social Workers in Rural Problem Area Counties, Summer of 1934,* (C-17). This study covered the following subjects: Number of visitors and cases per visitor, age and sex, salary, general education, social work training and experience, usual occupation and rural background. The study covered 355 supervisors and visitors who were serving 8,267 relief households. About one-third of the visitors and 27 per cent of the supervisors were men, and two-thirds and 73 per cent respectively were women. The average age of all social workers was about 35 years. The average monthly salary for visitors was $68.78 and for supervisors was $87.16. Forty-two per cent of the supervisors and 22 per cent of the visitors had had four years or more of college work, but three per cent of the supervisors and nine per cent of the visitors had had no formal education beyond grade school. Sixty-eight per cent of the supervisors and 91.5 per cent of the visitors had had no training or experience in social work, when training was defined as a course in case work or attendance at a school of social work and experience at social work employment outside of an emergency relief organization. Twenty per cent of the visitors had had no previous employed experience of any kind, and only six per cent reported social work as the usual occupation. More than 90 per cent of the visitors had previously lived in a small town or village or on a farm, and 91 per cent of the visitors and 66 per cent of the supervisors had formerly lived in the county in which they were working. Social workers appointed from outside the county in which they were working were on the average better educated and better trained than those appointed from within the county.

This study covers the social workers in 64 rural counties who were employed in the summer of 1934. It contains no comparative data for the pre-federal and the post-federal periods, but it does give highly useful information about the qualifications of this small selected group during a brief period. A national study covering the whole depression period is needed in order to see the changes in personnel qualifications and to get a more complete picture of all problems of personnel administration.

Appendix and Bibliographies

BIBLIOGRAPHIES of materials relating to the administration of relief are numerous but always limited in scope. They are valuable chiefly as a means of making a quick survey of what has been written about relief; many of the titles published had only ephemeral importance, but the perusal of a considerable number of them serves to give a general impression of the principal problems which have occupied the minds of those who have written articles, pamphlets and books on various aspects of relief policies and administration. The following bibliographies should be useful to anyone who undertakes a research project in the field covered by this monograph:

1. LIST OF BIBLIOGRAPHIES

Bulletin. Nos. 104, 105, 107, 109, 112, 113, 116, 117, 119, 120, 124, 125, 127, 130, 136, 137, 139 and 141. New York: Russell Sage Foundation: Library

Catalogue of Research Bulletins. Je 1 '36. Washington: Federal Emergency Relief Administration, Division of Research, Statistics, and Finance. '36

Catalogue of United States Documents, 1933-1937. Washington: Government Printing Office. '33-'37

Cumulative Book Index, 1929-1937, United States Catalogue Supplement. New York: The H. W. Wilson Co. See under (1) Charities and (2) Relief

Digest of Publications. Washington: Works Progress Administration and National Youth Administration, Division of Information and Publications. Ja 1 '36

Index of Monthly Reports. Washington: Federal Emergency Relief Administration. Je '33-'36

International Index to Periodicals, 1929-1937. New York: The H. W. Wilson Co. See under (1) Relief, (2) Unemployment, (3) Charities, (4) Public charities, (5) Social welfare, (6) Social workers, (7) Social work

Monthly Labor Review, 1929-1937. United States Department of Labor, Washington. See section entitled "Recent Publications of Labor Interest"

New York Times Index, 1929-1937. New York: New York Times Publishing Co. See under (1) Unemployment, (2) New York City Emergency Relief Bureau, (3) New York Temporary Emergency Relief Administration, (4) Charities, (5) Works Progress Administration, (6) Public Works Administration, (7) Civil Works Administration, (8) Relief

Public Welfare News. Vols. I-V. Chicago: American Public Welfare Association. See monthly issues for articles and book notes

Reader's Guide to Periodical Literature. New York: The H. W. Wilson Co. '29-'37. See under (1) Relief, (2) Unemployment, (3) Charities, (4) Public charities, (5) Social welfare, (6) Social workers, (7) Social work

Social Science Abstracts. Vols. I-IV. New York: Social Science Research Council. '29-'32. See under (1) Relief, (2) Mothers' aid, (3) Old age, (4) Old-age insurance, (5) Pensions, (6) Poor law, (7) Red Cross, (8) Social work, (9) Unemployment

Social Service Review. Chicago: University of Chicago Press. '29-'37. See sections entitled "Book Reviews" and "Public Documents"

Social Work Year Book. New York: Russell Sage Foundation. '29, '33, '35, '37

Subject Index of Research Bulletins and Monographs. Federal Emergency Relief Administration and Works Progress Administration, Division of Research, July, 1936

Survey, 1929-1937. New York: Survey Associates, Inc. See section entitled "Book Reviews"

This list of bibliographies is by no means exhaustive, but it is the opinion of the authors that it contains the most important titles for the research worker who is interested in the problems outlined in this monograph. Reference also should be made to the very extensive card index and abstracts of relief studies in the library of the Works Progress Administration in Washington, D.C.

2. A SELECTED LIST OF REPORTS AND STUDIES

There are many state and federal reports and sample studies of problems associated with the administration of relief during the depression. Most of these are ephemeral, but a few of them are of sufficient scope to warrant listing. No attempt has been made to list all of the worthwhile studies which have been made and published--the time available for the preparation of this monograph did not permit any such careful examination of them. The list given below contains some of the most important titles, and is intended to be suggestive. Titles mentioned in the body of the report are not repeated here. By far the largest number of studies of relief administration have been done either by or under the direction of the Federal Emergency Relief Administration and the Works Progress Administration.

The selected list of references is as follows:

Abbott, Edith, Breckinridge, S. P. *et al. The Tenements of Chicago.* Chicago: Univ. of Chicago Press. '36

Beck, P. G. and Forster, M. C. *Six Rural Problem Areas.* Washington: FERA. '35

Briggs, Alfred W. *The General Relief Problem.* Wisconsin Public Welfare Dept. '36

Cadbury, Olive C. *Social Work in Seattle*. Seattle: Seattle Community Fund. '35

California State Relief Administration. *Handbook of Consumers' Cooperatives in California.* '35

Connecticut Unemployment Commission. *Experience of the Emergency Relief Commission with Relief Administration in Connecticut.* '37

Elizabeth McCormick Memorial Fund. *Family Food Studies.* Chicago

Emergency Conservation Work Organization. *Report.* '35

Haber, William, and Stanchfield, Paul L. *Unemployment Relief and Economic Security.* Lansing, Mich.: State Emergency Welfare Relief Comm. *Second Report.*

Hathway, Marion, and Rademaker, John A. *Public Relief in Washington, 1853-1933.* No. 1. Olympia: Washington State Emergency Relief Administration. '34

Illinois Emergency Relief Commission. *Reports*

Indiana Governor's Commission on Unemployment Relief. *Year Book.* 1935

Kahn, Dorothy C. *Unemployment and Its Treatment in the United States.* New York: American Association of Social Workers. '37

Lanpher, Henry Coe. "The Civilian Conservation Corps: Some Aspects of Its Social Program for Unemployed Youth." *Social Service Review.* D '36

McCord, Elizabeth, van Dusseldorp, Wilma, and Pease, Sybil. *The State Department's Responsibility for the Development of Social Work Practice in Rural Areas.* Washington: FERA. '36

McCormick, Thomas C. *Rural Households, Relief and Non-Relief.* Washington: WPA. '35

Massoth, Leona E. "Some Current Misconceptions concerning Non-Residents." *Social Service Review.* Je '36

New York Governor's Commission on Unemployment Relief. *State and Local Welfare Organization in the State of New York.* '36

News Releases, 1-1199. Works Program. Washington: WPA

News Releases, 1-1220. Washington: FERA

Palmer, Gladys L. and Wood, Katherine D. *Urban Workers on Relief.* Part I. Washington: WPA '36. (See also Part II by Wood, Katherine D. '36)

Philadelphia Emergency Relief Bureau. *How Much Rent Do Relief Families Pay?* '36

Steker, Margaret L., *Inter-City Difference in the Cost of Living.* Washington: WPA. '36

U. S. Federal Emergency Relief Administration
  FERA Monthly Reports. '33-'36
  General Relief Statistics. Ja 1 '36 *et seq.*
  The Occupational Characteristics of the Relief and Non-Relief Populations in Dayton, Ohio. '35
  Schooling of Transients and Resident Homeless. '35
  Some Types of Unemployability in Rural Relief Cases. '35
  Statistical Summary of Emergency Relief Activities, Ja '33 through D '35; pub. '37

U. S. President's Organization on Unemployment Relief. *Circulars, News Releases, etc.,* Ap '31-Ap '32 collected

U. S. Public Health Service. *National Health Survey.* Still in progress

U. S. Works Progress Administration:
  Migrant Families, '36
  Sources of Income of Former Urban Relief Cases. '36

Summary of Surveys of Job Refusals by Relief Clients Reported in Six Communities. '35

Survey of Cases Closed from State Emergency Relief Administration Rolls in Twelve New Jersey Communities. '36

Unemployable Relief Cases in Thirteen Selected Cities. '36

Usual Occupations of Workers Eligible for Works Program Employment in the United States, 1937, Preliminary ed.

Workers on Relief in the United States: A Census of Usual Occupations. Abridged ed. '37

Webb, John N. *The Transient Unemployed.* Washington: WPA '35

Wood, Helen. *Youth in Search of Jobs.* Washington: WPA '35

Index

Studies in the Social Aspects
of the Depression

AN ARNO PRESS/NEW YORK TIMES COLLECTION

Chapin, F. Stuart and Stuart A. Queen.
Research Memorandum on Social Work in the Depression. 1937.

Collins, Selwyn D. and Clark Tibbitts.
Research Memorandum on Social Aspects of Health in the Depression. 1937.

The Educational Policies Commission.
Research Memorandum on Education in the Depression. 1937.

Kincheloe, Samuel C.
Research Memorandum on Religion in the Depression. 1937.

Sanderson, Dwight.
Research Memorandum on Rural Life in the Depression. 1937.

Sellin, Thorsten.
Research Memorandum on Crime in the Depression. 1937.

Steiner, Jesse F.
Research Memorandum on Recreation in the Depression. 1937.

Stouffer, Samuel A. and Paul F. Lazarsfeld.
Research Memorandum on the Family in the Depression. 1937.

Thompson, Warren S.
Research Memorandum on Internal Migration in the Depression. 1937.

Vaile, Roland S.
Research Memorandum on Social Aspects of Consumption in the Depression. 1937.

Waples, Douglas.
Research Memorandum on Social Aspects of Reading in the Depression. 1937.

White, R. Clyde and Mary K. White.
Research Memorandum on Social Aspects of Relief Policies in the Depression. 1937.

Young, Donald.
Research Memorandum on Minority Peoples in the Depression. 1937.